DESIGNER'S CASEBOOK
Number 6

DESIGNER'S CASEBOOK Number 6

Prepared by the Editors of
Electronics

Sixth in a continuing series of selected Designer's Casebook sections of Electronics magazine. This edition includes Electronics issues from November 17, 1981 through November 30, 1982. Also included are feature articles and items from Engineer's Notebook of particular interest to the circuit designer.

Price $7.00

ISBN 0-07-600002-8

McGraw-Hill Publications Co.
1221 Avenue of the Americas
New York, New York 10020

CONTENTS

OPTOELECTRONICS

OSCILLATORS

POWER SUPPLIES

SIGNAL DETECTORS & DISCRIMINATORS

AMPLIFIERS

Pair of pnp/npn transistors form high-voltage amplifier

by H. F. Nissink
Electrical Engineering Department, University of Adelaide, Australia

This simple high-voltage amplifier circuit provides a large output voltage swing with low-current consumption and uses only a few components. Its 280-volt regulated supply produces an unclipped output of up to 260 v peak to peak. In addition, rise and fall times of the output for a square-wave input are 150 nanoseconds, and the no-load supply current is only 4 milliamperes.

The principle behind this circuit is just a simple transistor amplifier (a) employing collector feedback through resistor R_F. The dc output is approximately $V_{be} \times R_F/R_1$. The circuit has an active pull-down action, with pull-up through R_2. However, if R_2 is replaced with a pnp transistor in a similar circuit, the pull-up and pull-down are through the transistor.

This substitution is the basis for the circuit in (b). Its output-voltage level is theoretically determined by the 300-kilohm and 1.3-kΩ resistors and thus the ac circuit gain is approximately 300 kΩ/10 kΩ = 30. The power supply (± 10 v dc) for the current amplifier A_1 driving 2N5416 is isolated from the supply for A_2, which is driving the 2N3439.

The circuit has an input impedance of 5 kΩ and an output impedance of 2.4 kΩ. For the component values shown, the actual gain measures about 27, and the output over the frequency range of 1 kilohertz to 300 kHz is 260 v peak to peak (without clipping) and 100 v peak to peak at 1 megahertz. Because the amplifier is not short-circuit protected at the output, the regulated power supply is limited by the current. This high-voltage amplifier may drive capacitive-type transducers and be used for several other applications. ☐

High-voltage amplifier. A simple transistor amplifier (a) employs collector feedback with R_2. Resistor R_2 is replaced by a circuit similar to (a) but with a pnp transistor to form the basis for a high-voltage amplifier (b). The current amplifiers A_1 and A_2 driving 2N5416 and 2N3439 use separate power supplies of ± 10 V dc.

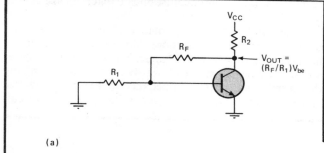

(a)

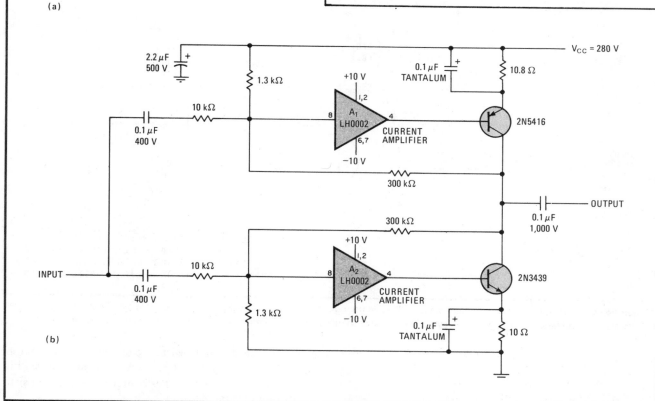

(b)

1

Exploiting the full potential
of an rf power transistor

by Dan Moline and Dan Bennett
Motorola Semiconductor Products Sector, Phoenix, Ariz.

With improved packaging and appropriate circuit design, the new MRF630 radio-frequency power transis-

tor can be used out to its design limits—the generation of 3 watts with 9.5 decibels of gain at ultrahigh frequencies when assembled with an all-gold metal system.

Good heat sinking enables Motorola's low-cost grounded-emitter TO-39 package for rf transistors to perform like a stripline opposed-emitter type. In this package, the MF630, also from Motorola, shows impressive boardband response, excellent heat dissipation, and high reliability.

So that heat can flow directly away from the transistor die, a flange is soldered to the bottom of the TO-39 can and secured to a heat sink by one or two screws (Fig. 1a). This assembly method maximizes heat dissipation while minimizing space requirements. Also, electrical grounding is better as the package is now connected mechanically to the chassis ground.

The broadband uhf amplifier circuit in Fig. 1b uses a distributed-element design to optimize the gain and bandwidth of the MRF630. The transmission lines are simulated by epoxy fiberglass G-10 board, whose high dielectric constant and low cost keep the circuit small and inexpensive. (In contrast, the commonly used glass Teflon board offers a low dielectric constant at a relatively high price.) To further cut the cost and exploit readily available components, mica capacitors are chosen for the matching network.

Broadband circuit performance (Fig. 2a) shows that the amplifier can furnish more than 3.0 w at frequencies in the range of 450 to 512 megahertz. The high power output can be extended above 490 MHz by optimizing the input and output–impedance-matching networks. With the addition of the copper flange in the circuit

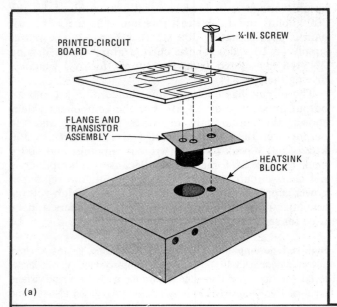

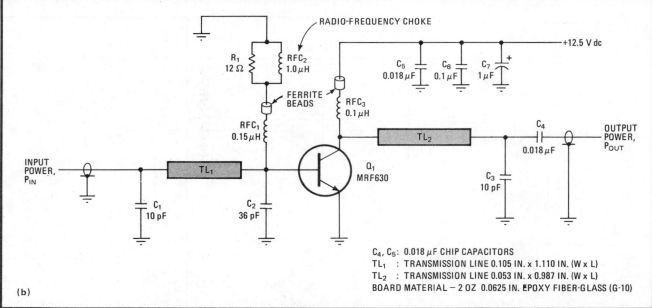

1. High power. Utilizing the construction technique outlined in (a), common emitter TO-39 package for Motorola's MRF630 provides excellent heat dissipation and reliability at high power levels. The amplifier (b) uses the distributed element design to obtain high power at uhf.

assembly, the thermal resistance of the transistor can be expected to be only 12° to 13°C/w. The gain curve (Fig. 2b) demonstrates typical performance of the transistor at ultrahigh frequencies. □

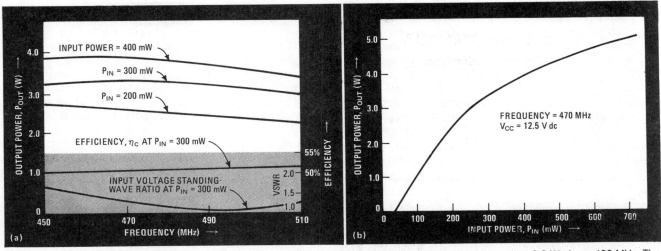

2. Broadband. Its high-frequency performance (a) shows that this amplifier can provide an output of more than 3.0 W above 490 MHz. The gain roll-off above 490 MHz is minimized by optimizing matching networks. The amplifier gain curve at 470 MHz is depicted in (b).

Current booster drives low-impedance load

by Jeffrey L. Sharp
NAP Consumer Electronics Corp., Knoxville, Tenn.

Successfully interfacing operational-amplifier circuitry with a low-impedance load is a common problem encountered by analog design engineers. This current booster offers a fix by employing bipolar power transistors that provide a compromise between maximum output voltage capability and effective device protection. However, the use of power MOS field-effect transistors in the output stage of the circuit current-limits the circuit and delivers output voltage approaching the supply.

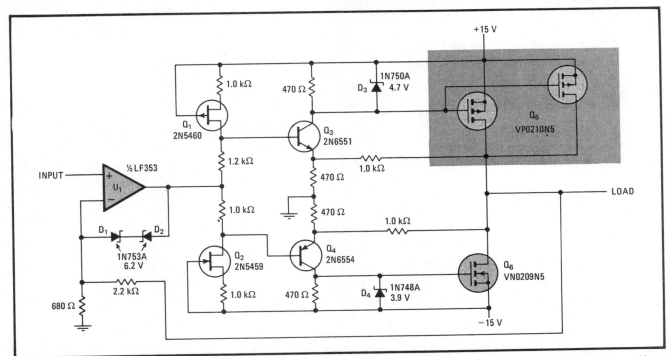

Low-impedance load. Using bipolar transistors and complementary power MOS FETs, this conjugate symmetry output circuit can drive a low-impedance load with high voltage and current over a wide range of frequencies. Matching FETs Q_5 and Q_6 reduce the distortion to less than 0.2% at 10 kHz and 0.03% at 1 kHz. Zener diodes D_3 and D_4 limit the output current.

The conjugate symmetry output stage of the booster (see figure) is composed of bipolar transistors and complementary power MOS FETs to provide a current booster that has a low output impedance and a high bandwidth. The use of power MOS FETs in the output section of the circuit prevents cross conduction at frequencies above 100 kilohertz. Because power MOS FETs Q_5 and Q_6 act together as a nearly ideal transconductance amplifier, zener diodes D_3 and D_4 effectively limit output current by setting the output's gate-source voltage according to

the relation: $V_z = V_{GSmax} = V_{GSth} + I_{Dmax}/g_{fs}$

where V_z = zener-diode voltage, V_{GSmax} = maximum gate-source voltage, V_{GSth} = gate-source threshold voltage, I_{Dmax} = maximum drain current and g_{fs} = common-source forward transconductance.

Careful device selection keeps the distortion at a minimum, especially in a class-B design. Because transconductance is a nonlinear function of drain current, the best selection method is a comparison of characteristic curves. Q_5 is composed of two p-channel MOS FETs that are connected in parallel. They effectively double this transistor's transconductance to 1 mho at a 1-ampere drain current and thereby match it to the n-channel MOS FET's transconductance of 0.9 mho at 2 A.

A 12.5-volt sine wave may be driven into an 8-ohm load from ±15-V supplies with the circuit, and a 20-Ω load may be driven to a 14-V peak. Its total harmonic distortion is 0.2% at 10 kHz and 0.03% at 1 kHz. In addition, its efficiency is 55% at full power and its output has a phase shift of about 10° at 100 kHz.

To ensure stability, the current-boosted amplifier must be operated at a gain that is greater than the output stage's voltage gain and must have careful component layout. Sufficient heat sinking is required to protect the amplifier from faulty loads that may result in a high output voltage at maximum current. Diodes D_1 and D_2 prevent op amp U_1 from saturating when the amp loop opens temporarily or the load is shorted. □

CONTROL CIRCUITS

Resistor-based servo replaces mechanical governors in motors

by John Gaewsky and Herbert Hardy
Polaroid Corp., Cambridge, Mass.

Mechanical governors in motors having two speed settings may now be replaced by an equally efficient feedback circuit that uses a resistor instead of a bulky and expensive transducer to sense motor speed. The circuit shrinks the motor's size without impairing its efficiency and also lengthens motor life, partially because it eliminates regulator-contact arcing. Only one integrated circuit and some discrete components are used. A light-emitting diode indicates an out-of-regulation state and the accompanying acceleration.

The servo system (a) measures the back electromotive force generated by the motor and uses it to generate an electrical signal proportional to the motor's speed. This

Servo control. The servo system in (a) allows a continuous speed adjustment of a electrically governed motor while retaining the efficiency of a mechanical governor. The circuitry in (b) uses only one IC (LM324) and few discrete components to emulate the mechanical governor. The circuit measures the back emf generated by the motor and uses it to generate an electrical signal proportional to the motor's speed. It also indicates out-of-regulation and acceleration.

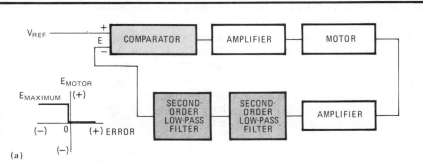

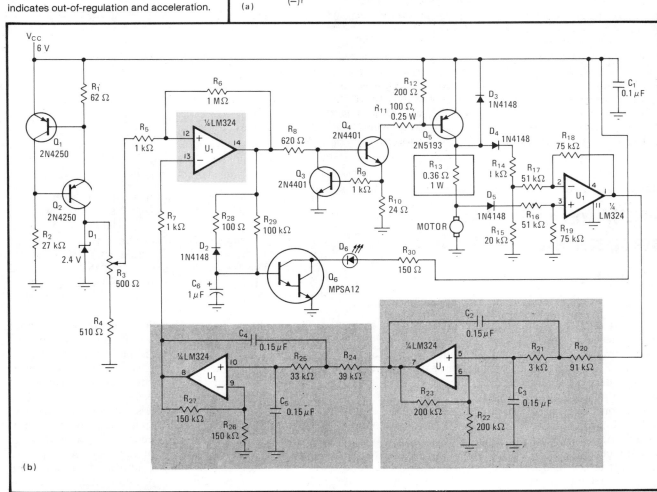

signal is then filtered by a four-pole low-pass active filter whose cutoff frequency is determined by the fundamental frequency of the brush noise at the motor's lowest controllable speed. The four-pole filter is obtained by cascading two second-order low-pass filters.

The filter output is compared with an adjustable reference, which is set by zener diode D_1 and adjusted using potentiometer R_3. When the speed signal is lower than the reference, power is applied to the motor, causing it to accelerate until the signal is greater than the reference. Because of the lag generated by the motor's time constant, the motor's speed response to an applied voltage is not immediate. The power that is switched to the motor is controlled by the comparator output. To limit the driver current, a low-power switching circuit is connected as a constant current source.

Sense resistor R_{13} is placed between V_{CC} and the armature resistance (R_a) of the motor in the speed-sensing circuit (b) and is used to form a bridge circuit satisfying the relationship $R_{14}/R_{15} = R_{13}/R_a$. This condition together with an appropriate gain of the amplifier, given by R_{18}/R_{17}, results in a differential voltage output that is proportional to the motor's speed. Losses in the sense resistor are minimized by selecting a value of $0.1R_a$ for it. In addition, diodes D_4 and D_5 prevent the input to the differential amplifier from exceeding the maximum specification.

When the motor is accelerating or the load-voltage variation requires a continuous power application (100% duty cycle), the out-of-regulation indicator lights. A duty cycle of less than 100% causes C_6 to discharge through R_{28}, which prevents Q_6 from turning on. □

PROM forms flexible stepper-motor controller

by Gregory C. Jewell
Caldisk, Provo, Utah

With just a 256-by-4-bit programmable read-only memory, a decoder, and a driver, this design provides a programmable stepper-motor controller. The example given here is a four-phase stepping motor incorporated in a floppy-disk drive. However, the idea is easily adapted to other applications.

The controller uses four of the PROM's eight input-address bits. They are connected to the outputs to obtain a stable state only when the input address—consisting of four direct and four feedback inputs—produces an output equal to the feedback address. Therefore, when one of the direct inputs changes state, the resulting output

changes in sequence until a stable state is attained.

A working version of the design (see figure) uses 1-K PROM 74S287, two-to-four-line decoder 25LS2539, and drivers Q_1 through Q_4. The four direct inputs are initialize ($\overline{INT}$), step ($\overline{ST}$), direction (DI) and track 00 (TRK 00). The feedback inputs are NSF, NDF, A_1F, and A_0F. In addition, the step input is a pulse generated by the rising edge of the step signal that is sent by the disk controller.

The direction of motor rotation is controlled by input DI, which determines the order of activation for the motor phases. TRK 00, which is provided by a sensor circuit, is active when the read/write head is positioned above it. In addition, the PROM does not allow the motor controller to step lower than TRK 00.

Two of the four output signals, NS and ND, indicate internal states and are also fed back to the input. Outputs A_1 and A_0 are decoded by U_{2-A}. This decoder output is used to control one of the four motor phases when the motor-enable input is active. The relationship between PROM outputs A_1, A_0, and motor phase is

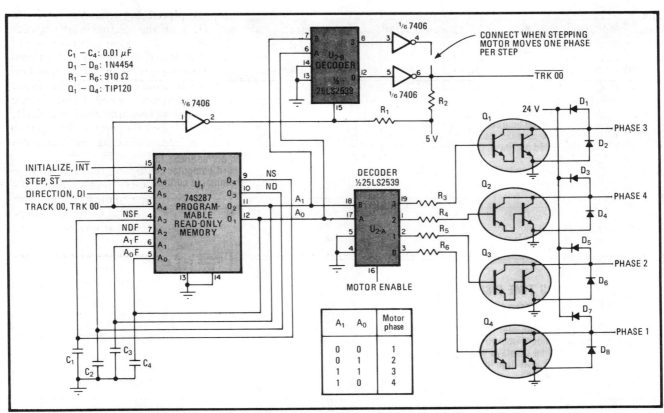

C_1 – C_4: 0.01 μF
D_1 – D_8: 1N4454
R_1 – R_6: 910 Ω
Q_1 – Q_4: TIP120

Controller. The stepper-motor controller employs a 256-by-4-bit programmable read-only memory, a decoder, and drivers Q_1 through Q_4. Decoder U_{2-B} is provided for track 00 detection. The chart illustrates the relationship between A_1, A_0, and the motor phases.

A_1	A_0	Motor phase
0	0	1
0	1	2
1	1	3
1	0	4

TABLE 1: STEPPER-MOTOR TRUTH TABLE TO MOVE TWO PHASES PER STEP												
Inputs								**Outputs**				**Comments**
$\overline{\text{INT}}$	DI	$\overline{\text{ST}}$	TRK 00	NSF	NDF	A_1F	A_0F	NS	ND	A_1	A_0	
0	X	X	X	X	X	X	X	0	0	0	0	initialization
1	X	1	X	0	0	0	0	0	0	0	0	stable at even track
1	0	0	1	0	0	0	0	0	0	0	0	cannot step lower than track 00
1	0	0	0	0	0	0	0	0	1	0	0	step to lower intermediate phase state
1	X	0	X	0	1	0	0	1	1	0	0	
1	X	0	X	1	1	0	0	1	1	0	1	
1	X	0	X	1	1	0	1	1	1	0	1	stable at intermediate phase state
1	X	1	X	1	1	0	1	0	1	0	1	step to lower (odd) track
1	X	X	X	0	1	0	1	0	0	0	1	
1	X	X	X	0	0	0	1	0	0	1	1	
1	X	1	X	0	0	1	1	0	0	1	1	stable at odd track
1	0	X	X	0	0	1	1	0	1	1	1	step to lower intermediate phase state
1	X	0	X	0	1	1	1	1	1	1	1	
1	X	0	X	1	1	1	1	1	1	1	0	
1	X	0	X	1	1	1	0	1	1	1	0	stable at intermediate phase state
1	X	1	X	1	1	1	0	0	1	1	0	step to lower (even) track
1	X	X	X	0	1	1	0	0	0	1	0	
1	X	X	X	0	0	1	0	0	0	0	0	
1	X	1	X	0	0	0	0	0	0	0	0	stable at even track
1	1	0	X	0	0	0	0	1	0	0	0	step to higher intermediate phase state
1	X	0	X	1	0	0	0	1	0	0	0	
1	X	0	X	1	0	1	0	1	0	1	0	stable at intermediate phase state
1	X	1	X	1	0	1	0	1	0	1	1	step to higher (odd) track
1	X	1	X	1	0	1	1	0	0	1	1	
1	X	1	X	0	0	1	1	0	0	1	1	stable at odd track
1	1	0	X	0	0	1	1	1	0	1	1	step to higher intermediate phase state
1	X	0	X	1	0	1	1	1	0	0	1	
1	X	0	X	1	0	0	1	1	0	0	1	stable at intermediate phase state
1	X	1	X	1	0	0	1	1	0	0	0	step to higher (even) track
1	X	1	X	1	0	0	0	0	0	0	0	
1	X	1	X	0	0	0	0	0	0	0	0	stable at even track
1	X	1	X	0	1	0	0	0	0	0	0	define invalid states
1	X	1	X	0	1	1	1	0	0	1	1	
1	X	1	X	1	1	0	0	1	0	0	0	
1	X	1	X	1	1	1	1	1	0	1	1	
				1 = HIGH		0 = LOW		X = DON'T CARE				

TABLE 2: STEPPER-MOTOR TRUTH TABLE TO MOVE ONE PHASE PER STEP

Inputs								Outputs				Comments
$\overline{INT}$	DI	$\overline{ST}$	TRK 00	NSF	NDF	A_1F	A_0F	NS	ND	A_1	A_0	
0	X	X	X	X	X	X	X	1	1	0	1	initialization at odd track
1	X	1	X	1	1	0	1	1	1	0	1	
1	X	0	X	1	1	0	1	1	1	0	0	step to higher (even) track
1	X	0	X	1	1	0	0	0	1	0	0	
1	X	0	X	0	1	0	0	0	1	0	0	stable at even track (see state 5)
1	X	1	X	0	0	0	0	0	0	0	0	state 1: stable at even track
1	0	0	1	0	0	0	0	0	0	0	0	cannot step lower than track 00
1	0	0	0	0	0	0	0	1	0	0	0	step to lower (odd) track
1	0	0	X	1	0	0	0	1	0	0	1	
1	X	0	X	1	0	0	1	1	0	0	1	state 2: stable at odd track
1	X	1	X	1	0	0	1	0	0	0	1	enable next step sequence
1	X	1	X	0	0	0	1	0	0	0	1	stable at odd track
1	0	0	X	0	0	0	1	0	1	0	1	step to lower (even) track
1	0	0	X	0	1	0	1	0	1	1	1	
1	X	0	X	1	1	1	1	0	1	1	1	state 3: stable at even track
1	X	1	X	0	1	1	1	0	0	1	1	enable next step sequence
1	X	1	X	0	0	1	1	0	0	1	1	stable at even track
1	0	0	1	0	0	1	1	0	0	1	1	cannot step lower than track 00
1	0	0	0	0	0	1	1	1	0	1	1	step to lower (odd) track
1	0	0	X	1	0	1	1	1	0	1	0	
1	X	0	X	1	0	1	0	1	0	1	0	state 4: stable at odd track
1	X	1	X	1	0	1	0	0	0	1	0	enable next step sequence
1	X	1	X	0	0	1	0	0	0	1	0	stable at odd track
1	0	0	X	0	0	1	0	0	1	1	0	step to lower (even) track
1	0	0	X	0	1	1	0	0	1	0	0	
1	X	0	X	0	1	0	0	0	1	0	0	state 5: stable at even track
1	X	1	X	0	1	0	0	0	0	0	0	enable next step sequence
1	X	1	X	0	0	0	0	0	0	0	0	stable at even track (see state 1)
1	1	0	X	0	0	0	0	1	0	0	0	step to higher (odd) track
1	1	0	X	1	0	0	0	1	0	1	0	
1	X	0	X	1	0	1	0	1	0	1	0	stable at odd track (see state 4)
1	1	0	X	0	0	1	0	0	1	1	0	step to higher (even) track
1	1	0	X	0	1	1	0	0	1	1	1	
1	X	0	X	0	1	1	1	0	1	1	1	stable at even track (see state 3)
1	1	0	X	0	0	1	1	1	0	1	1	step to higher (odd) track
1	1	0	X	1	0	1	1	1	0	0	1	
1	X	0	X	1	0	0	1	1	0	0	1	stable at odd track (see state 2)
1	1	0	X	0	0	0	1	0	1	0	1	step to higher (even) track
1	1	0	X	0	1	0	1	0	1	0	0	
1	X	0	X	0	1	0	0	0	1	0	0	stable at even track (see state 5)
1	0	1	X	0	1	0	1	0	0	0	1	define invalid states
1	1	1	X	0	1	0	1	0	0	0	1	
1	0	1	X	0	1	1	0	0	0	1	0	
1	1	1	X	0	1	1	0	0	0	1	0	
1	0	1	X	1	0	0	0	0	0	0	0	
1	1	1	X	1	0	0	0	0	0	0	0	
1	0	1	X	1	0	1	1	0	0	1	1	
1	1	1	X	1	0	1	1	0	0	1	1	
1	X	1	X	1	1	0	0	0	1	0	0	
1	X	X	X	1	1	1	0	1	0	1	0	
1	X	X	X	1	1	1	1	0	1	1	1	

1 = HIGH   0 = LOW   X = DON'T CARE

shown in the figure. The decoder $U_{2\text{-}B}$ generates $\overline{TRK\ 00}$ to enable the drive interface only when the proper motor phase exists.

Tables 1 and 2 show the functioning of the circuit in mode 1 and mode 2, respectively. Mode 1 moves the motor two phases per step. In this mode, the motor is adjusted to position the read/write head above the even tracks when phase 1 is active and above the odd tracks when phase 3 is active. In mode 2, which moves the motor one phase a step, the motor is adjusted to position the read/write head above even tracks when phase 1 or phase 3 is active. An active phase 2 or phase 4 indicates odd-numbered tracks. A power-on problem is overcome by initializing the stepper motor at an odd track and automatically stepping to the next higher even track. □

Phase-reversal protector trips main contactor

by Leuridan Carty
Lima, Peru

When the direction of phase rotation is critical, as in a three-phase motor, the reversal of two phases can cause disastrous damage. The advantage of this low-cost phase-reversal protector is that it is independent of line frequency and requires no transformers. Only one chip and few discrete components are needed for the simple circuit, which can also be easily modified to obtain a phase-sequence detector.

The line voltage is directly sensed and applied through transistors Q_1 and Q_2 to the data and clock inputs of flip-flop U_1 (see figure). The reversal of one or more input phases produces a reset pulse at output $\overline{Q}_1$ of U_1. This is delayed by 1 second by means of R_1 and C_1 and then is fed into flip-flop U_2. U_2 is now reset to produce an output at Q_2, which is used to drive triac Q_3 into an off-state, so that the main contactor is disabled and the equipment protected.

The phase-sequence detector is obtained by connecting U_1 and U_2 in parallel and by feeding the Q and $\overline{Q}$ outputs to two light-emitting diodes. A normally open push-button switch is connected in series with input phase T. If this switch is pressed, one of the LEDs glows, indicating the direction of input phases. The Q output corresponds to clockwise rotation and $\overline{Q}$ to anticlockwise. □

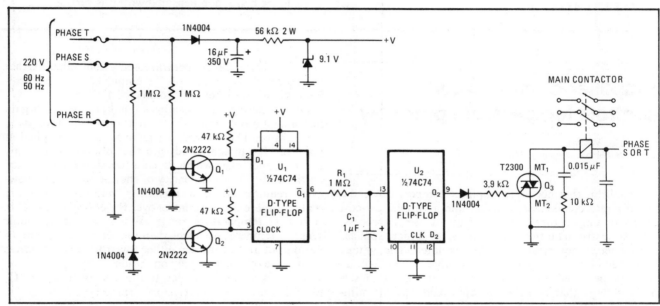

Protection. The circuit links D-type flip-flop 74C74, triac T2300, and a few discrete components into a simple, low-cost phase-reversal protector. Reversal of one or more input phases enables triac Q_3, which is turn disables the main contactor and protects the equipment.

Improved design optimizes three-mode controller

by Manuel R. Cereijo
Florida International University, Miami, Fla.

For certain processes, one- or two-mode controls can not handle sudden large load changes. So in order to keep the error within acceptable limits, a proportional integral derivative controller is used. The derivative mode produces an anticipatory action that reduces the maximum error caused by sudden load changes, and the integral mode provides a reset action that eliminates proportional offset. However, this modified version improves the performance of the controller without extra cost or an operational amplifier. The start-up, overdriving, and switching problems associated with the traditional controller are avoided with this design.

A general equation defining the ideal three-mode controller is written as:

$$m_1(t) = K_p e + \left(\frac{K_p}{T_i} \int e \, dt \right) + K_p T_d \frac{de}{dt} + m_0$$

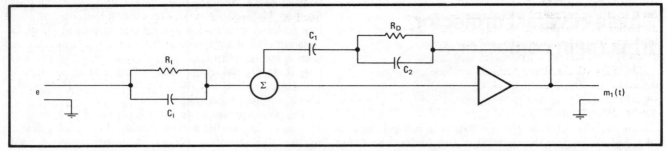

Controller. This modified proportional integral derivative controller improves the performance of a traditional configuration without adding operational amplifiers to the circuit. The design modifies the basic equation by rearranging the integral and derivative terms in series.

where e = the input, K_p = proportional gain, T_i = integral action time, T_d = derivative action time, m_1 = controller output, and m_0 = controller output with no input. If the integral and derivative terms are written in series m(t) may be expressed as:

$$K_p\left(1+\frac{T_d}{T_i}\right)\left(e+\left[\frac{1}{T_d+T_i}\int e\,dt\right]+\frac{T_dT_i}{T_d+T_i}\frac{de}{dt}\right)+m_0$$

The derivative action is formed at the input, and the integral action is formed in the feedback loop. Also, fast signals are better compensated with this version. □

Amplifier-compensator controls temperature precisely

by Charles Whiting
Analog Devices Inc., Wilmington, Mass.

A monolithic thermocouple amplifier-compensator and a few discrete components can become a simple low-cost set-point temperature-control circuit of use in process-control instrumentation, appliances, or other applications where temperature must be regulated. The voltage produced by a type-J thermocouple is cold-junction–compensated and compared with an external set-point voltage that is scaled to approximately 10 milli-volts per °C for the temperature being controlled. (Other thermocouple types can also be employed if proper scaling resistors are externally connected.)

Disconnecting the feedback makes the high-gain instrumentation amplifier section of U_1 behave as a comparator. The external set-point voltage is applied at pin 8 of U_1 and compared with the voltage produced by the thermocouple, which is cold-junction–compensated on the chip. The nonlinearity of the thermocouple, however, requires using a nonlinear voltage-temperature scale for more precise control over the entire −200° C to +760° C temperature range. When the thermocouple senses a temperature lower than the set point, the amplifier output at V_o is driven either toward zero or negative in the case of a dual-supply operation.

This low signal is applied to the base of transistor Q_1 through the 20-kilohm resistor, turning Q_1 off and Q_2 on,

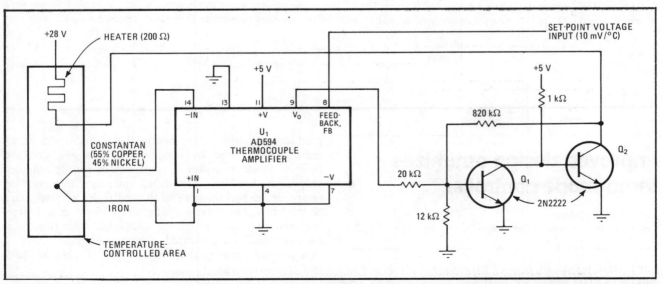

Thermal control. The voltage developed by the cold-junction–compensated thermocouple is compared with the external set-point voltage that is scaled to approximately 10 mV/°C for the temperature being controlled. This external voltage is applied to pin 8 of thermocouple amplifier U_1. The circuit is capable of providing a precise control over a wide temperature range.

so that current flows into the heater. When the temperature in the controlled area exceeds the set point, the amplifier is overdriven in the positive direction. This high positive signal turns Q_2 off by turning Q_1 on, and as a result the current to the heater is shut off.

The 820-kΩ feedback resistor connected between the collector of Q_2 and base of Q_1 speeds up the on-off switching of Q_2 and thereby minimizes the transistor power dissipation. When Q_2 turns on and its collector voltage begins to drop, the drop in voltage is coupled back to the base of Q_1 through the 820-kΩ resistor. As the base of Q_1 is now driven low, the voltage on its collector and the base of Q_2 rises, further reducing the latter's collector voltage and speeding its cutoff.

If the circuit employed a relay to switch large amounts of current to the heating element, it could control a high-power heating element or its output could serve as a high-low signal for a temperature alarm circuit. □

Switching circuit fulfills three functions

by Charles Carson
WASH-FM, Metromedia Radio, Washington, D. C.

With just a single switching system, one audio processor may be shared by many different recording stations. The system can without noise or interference switch the processor to the station where it is needed, cancels its use at the locations where it is not being employed, and identifies its switching mode. As an example, the circuit is set up for three stations, but more functions can be added by using extra identical stages.

The output of the alternate-action switch consisting of inverters U_{1-a} and U_{1-b} changes state once S_1 is closed or optocoupler O_1 is turned on (Fig. 1). When the alternate-action switch's output at pin 4 is high, transistor Q_4 is turned on and relay 1 is energized. Also, this high output resets the other two alternate-action switches, turning them off. Closing S_1 again makes the output at pin 4 of U_{1-b} go low. As a result, relay 1 is disabled.

When station 1 is on, so is its corresponding lamp. The

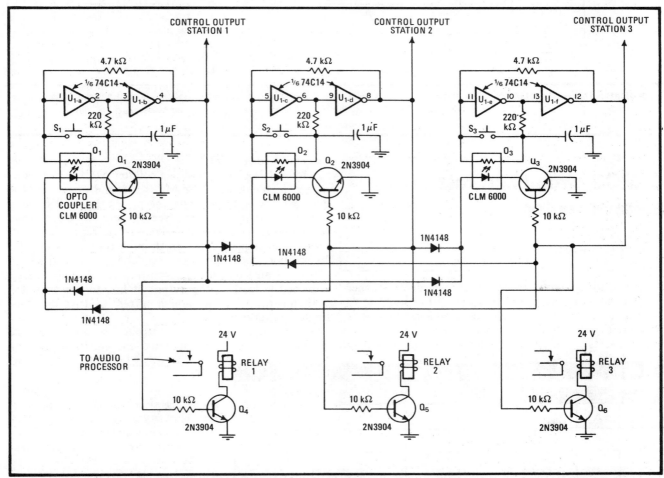

1. Switching. By means of this circuit, a single audio processor can switch between three recording stations. Inverters U_{1-a} and U_{1-b} form the alternate-action switch for station 1. Similarly inverters U_{1-c} through U_{1-f} simulate the switching action for stations 2 and 3. Relay 1 is energized when the output at pin 4 of U_{1-b} is high. In addition, this output resets the other two switches.

lamps for stations 2 and 3 flash to indicate that the system is in use elsewhere (Fig. 2). All the lamps are off when the system is not in use.

Inverters U$_{2-a}$ and U$_{2-b}$ form an astable oscillator operating at 1 hertz. Because transistor Q$_7$ is turned on when station 1 is on, the station's lamp burns continuously. The logic high is diode-coupled to AND gates U$_{3-b}$ and

U$_{3-c}$ and now allows the output of the astable oscillator to be fed to transistors Q$_8$ and Q$_9$ through the gates and the diodes. This transistor output makes the lamps at the other two stations flash at 1 Hz. When the stations are idle, the control lines are in a low state, and consequently the indicator lamps remain off. □

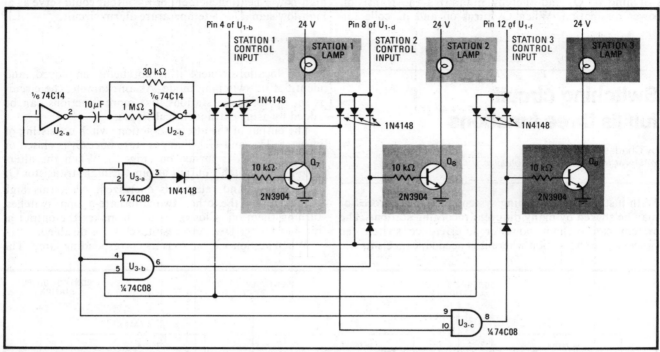

2. Indicator. This section of the circuit contains three lamps to indicate the switching mode. When station 1 is on, transistor Q$_7$ is activated and the lamp in its collector path burns continuously. The other two lamps flash at a frequency determined by oscillator U$_{2-a}$ through U$_{2-b}$.

C-MOS circuit controls stepper motor

by Otto Neumann
Square D Canada, Waterloo, Ont., Canada

Of the many circuits around that can drive stepper motors, this stepper controller is one of the simplest to construct. It uses just a few popular complementary-MOS integrated circuits and Darlington power transistors, its cost is low, its power consumption is minimal, and it may

be controlled remotely.

Motorola's binary up-down counter MC14516 is connected to binary decoder MC14555 and quadruple OR gate MC14071 to generate the pulses that will drive a four-phase stepping motor (see figure). The clock input to counter U$_1$ runs at 120 hertz and is derived from a 555 timer. The stepper is driven through transistors Q$_1$–Q$_4$. In addition, each output of decoder U$_{2-a}$ drives the base of each transistor through resistors R$_3$–R$_6$. This setup reduces the load on the output of U$_{2-a}$ to less than 1.3 milliamperes, which is enough current to drive the Darlington power device.

The motor's rotation is controlled by switch S$_1$. A +12-volt dc source is supplied to pin 10 of U$_1$ for

TRUTH TABLE FOR CLOCKWISE ROTATION									
Counter output		Decoder output				Motor terminal			
B	A	Q$_3$	Q$_2$	Q$_1$	Q$_0$	5	1	4	3
0	0	0	0	0	1	1	1	0	0
0	1	0	0	1	0	0	1	1	0
1	0	0	1	0	0	0	0	1	1
1	1	1	0	0	0	1	0	0	1

Driver. This stepper-motor driver uses complementary-MOS integrated circuits and Darlington power transistors to control the speed and direction of the stepper's rotation. Up-down counter MC14516 is linked with decoder MC14555 and quad OR gate MC14071 to generate the pulses for driving the motor through transistors Q$_1$–Q$_4$. The unit can be controlled remotely.

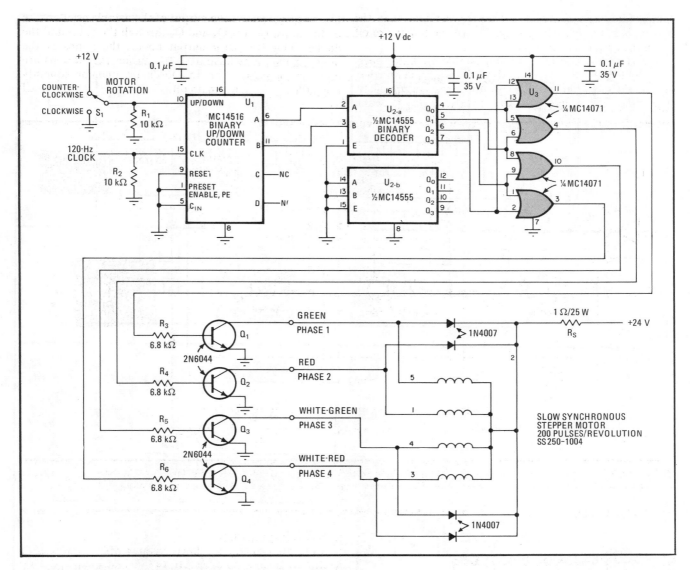

counterclockwise rotation; grounding pin 10 gives clockwise rotation. Unused section U_{2-b} of the decoder is grounded to shield the IC from transients. Pull-down resistors are recommended when the clock input and the clockwise-counterclockwise selection switch are located more than 1 foot from the driver board.

With a high-torque motor, such as an SS250-1004 with a torque of 225 ounce-inch, sensing resistor R_s must be employed. This resistor protects the stepper motor. With a low-torque motor, about 50 oz-in., it is not necessary to use R_s, and the motor supply should be reduced to +14 v dc. □

Serial-communication link controls remote displays

by John Klimek
Pretoria, South Africa

This simple serial-communication circuit provides a remote control for a four-digit display through a two-wire communication link. The transmitter converts parallel input data into serial output data in the form of long and short pulses representing the high and low levels of the shift-register output, respectively, while the receiver decodes the serial input data for the display circuitry. The circuit is useful for applications requiring low-cost remote display units.

The binary-coded decimal data is entered into U_1 and U_2, the two 8-bit shift registers of the transmitter (a). This data is shifted out in accordance with pulse train M (b), which is generated by counter U_3. The counter is driven by a 2-kilohertz square-wave oscillator, which is composed of a CD4093 Schmitt trigger, a 10-nanofarad capacitor, and a 100-kilohm resistor. Depending on the state of output Q_8 of register U_1, waveform M is converted into either 320-microsecond or 100-μs pulses.

On receiving these pulses, dual 4-bit register U_4 and

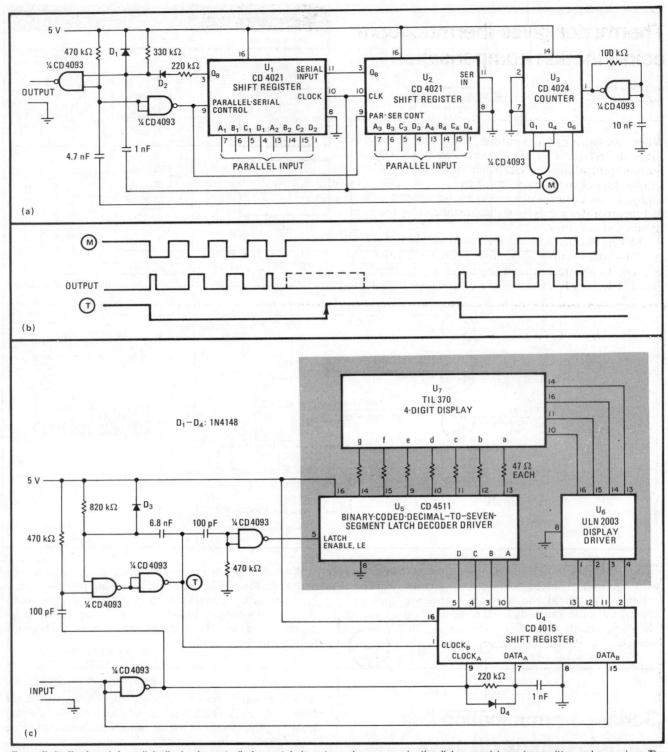

Four-digit display. A four-digit display is controlled remotely by a two-wire communication link comprising a transmitter and a receiver. The transmitter section (a) converts BCD data into high and low bits at the output of shift register U_1. These bits are then transformed into short and long pulses (b) at the transmitter output. The receiver (c) decodes the input pulses for the display circuitry.

the timing network at its input convert the pulses into high- or low-level bits (c). The data is transferred in groups of four pulses and entered into the internal latches of U_5 at the positive edge of pulse-train T. This train also clocks the other half of U_4. The B section of U_4 generates a high-level pulse in sequence, which enables

the desired character via driver U_6 to be in phase with the segment-enabling pulses generated by the A section of U_4. After every 16 data pulses, converted into 4 output pulses, a fifth pulse is generated by Q_6 of U_3, as is shown on the timing diagram. The high-level bit is then recorded from this pulse. □

Thermistor gives thermocouple cold-junction compensation

by Harry L. Trietle,
Yellow Springs Instruments Co., Yellow Springs, Ohio

RESISTOR VALUES FOR COMPENSATING THERMOCOUPLE COLD-JUNCTIONS		
Thermocouple	R_2 (±0.1%)	R_4 (±0.1%)
Type E	46.03 Ω	23.66 Ω
Type J	39.02 Ω	19.88 Ω
Type K	30.51 Ω	15.53 Ω
Type T	30.66 Ω	15.86 Ω

Thermistor = YSI 44006 (18.79 kΩ at 10°C, 10.00 kΩ at 25°C, 5.592 kΩ at 40°)
V_{REF} = 1.000 V ±0.1%, R_1 = 7.15 kΩ ±0.1%, R_3 = 20.0 kΩ ±0.1%

When measuring temperatures with thermocouples, either the reference or cold junction must be held at a constant temperature or electronic compensation for the temperature changes is needed at the cold junction. This cold-junction compensator (a) uses the latter approach and incorporates a precision thermistor having high sensitivity and accuracy.

The heart of the device is the thermistor bridge circuit (b). The thermistor's nonlinearity characteristics are balanced by the resistance bridge, and with the proper choice of R_1 and R_2, the bridge's output closely matches that of the reference junction. The total series resistance of R_1 and R_2 necessary for a linearized bridge circuit is calculated by using the following equation:

$$R_1 + R_2 = \frac{R_{10}R_{25} + R_{25}R_{40} - 2R_{10}R_{40}}{R_{10} + R_{40} - 2R_{25}}$$

where R_{10}, R_{25}, and R_{40} are the thermistor's resistances at 10°, 25°, and 40° C, respectively.

With the resulting values of R_1 and R_2, the voltage

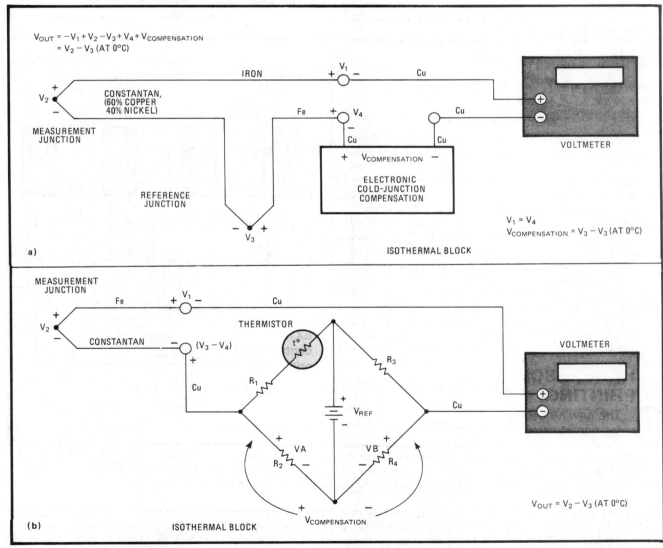

Compensation. The cold-junction compensator used in the general scheme (a) for thermocouple measurements is based on the thermistor bridge circuit (b). R_1 and R_2 must be selected so that the bridge output is near the reference junction's potential. The compensator's error is substantially reduced by using resistors and a bridge voltage accurate to 0.1%.

drops across them between 10° and 25° C are the same as from 25° to 40° C. The average temperature sensitivity is then determined by calculating the voltage drop across $R_1 + R_2$ between 10° and 40° C. R_2 is selected so that the sensitivities of the thermocouple and V_A are equalized.

The table gives component values for the four most popular thermocouple types when a reference voltage of 1.000 volt is applied and a 10-kilohm precision thermistor is used in the bridge circuit. The thermistor's high sensitivity of about 4%/°C and ±0.2° C accuracy makes possible precise electrical compensation without calibration. The compensator's error may be substantially reduced by using resistors and a bridge voltage in the circuit that are accurate to 0.1%. The error in this case is less than ±0.55°C between 10°C and 40°C. □

C-MOS ICs make precise digital timer

by Otto Neumann
Square D Canada, Waterloo, Ont., Canada

This digital timer (see figure) uses readily available complementary-MOS integrated circuits for low power consumption. It is simple and precise, and its timing sequences are set with four thumbwheel switches. Adding more frequency dividers to the clock input can extend the range from seconds to minutes to hours.

When the jumper on pin 11 of U_{2-a} is tapped, the input frequency of 60 or 50 hertz is applied to U_{2-a}, which divides it by 6 or 5, respectively. U_{2-b} further divides it by 10 to provide a pulse every second to the input of U_{3-c}. The timer starts counting down as soon as start switch S_1 is pressed. When counter U_1 reaches 0000, the low output on its pin 2 resets the flip-flop comprising U_{3-a} and U_{3-b}, whose output in turn energizes relay K_1. The counter now reads the thumbwheel setting and shows it on the display.

When the counter starts counting, any changes in the thumbwheel setting will not affect the selected time because the counter is already loaded. Only after reset push button S_2 is pressed does the counter stop counting and return to the new setting. Transistor Q_1 and its components protect the reset input, which is susceptible to noise. Diodes D_4–D_{19} prevent crosstalk between the thumbwheel switches connected in parallel.

The internal oscillator frequency is 10 kilohertz and the scan cycle time is 400 microseconds when no capacitor is connected to pin 13 of U_1. The frequency can be reduced to 1 kHz by connecting a 90-picofarad capacitor from pin 13 to ground, causing the scan cycle time to increase. The common cathode display can be changed to a common-anode version by replacing U_1 with ICM7217IJI and reversing each of the D_4–D_{19} diodes. □

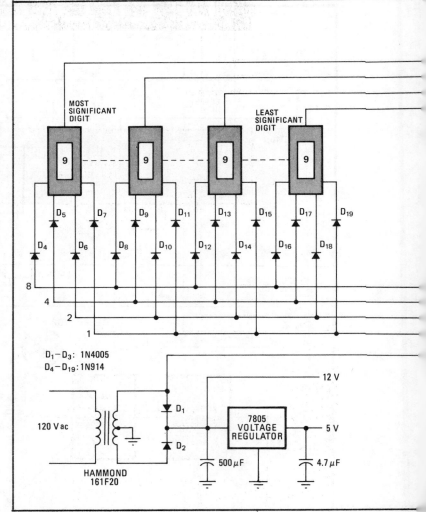

Timer. This digital timer uses C-MOS integrated circuits U_1 through U_3 to lower circuit power consumption. Frequency divider U_2 reduces the input frequency to 1 hertz, which is gated with flip-flop output to clock counter U_1. Thumbwheel switches set the desired time in seconds for the timer, which is initiated by pressing switch S_1.

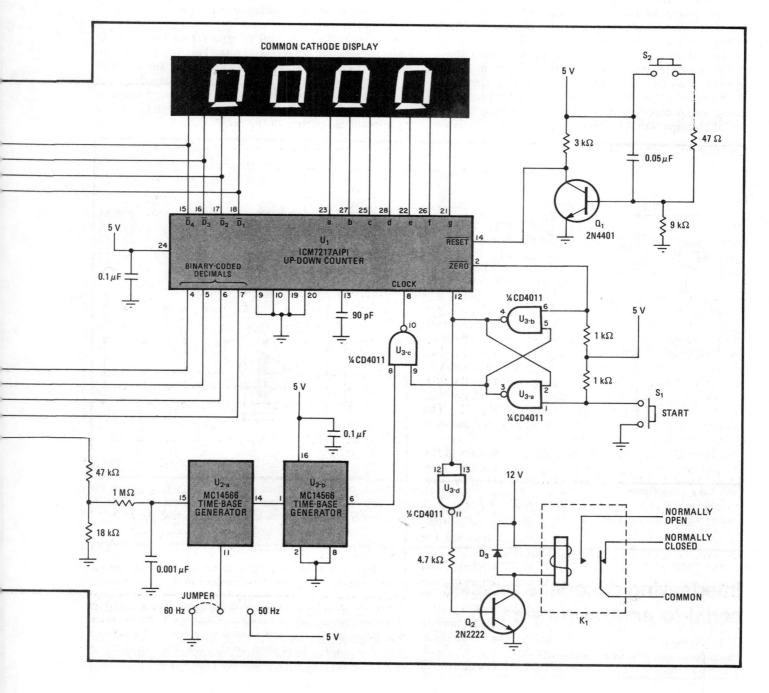

CONVERTER CIRCUITS

Two-chip VCO linearly controls ramp's amplitude and frequency

by Forrest P. Clay Jr. and Mark S. Eaton
Department of Physics, Old Dominion University, Norfolk, Va.

This inexpensive ramp generator provides a proportional voltage control of both the period and amplitude of a waveform over a wide range and thus doubles as a linear voltage-to-frequency converter. Only a few active devices are needed: two operational amplifiers and a transistor.

Two dc differential control signals, V_{f_1} and V_{f_2}, are applied to op amps A_1 and A_2. The output from A_3 is $V_{C_1} + (V_{f_1} - V_{f_2}) = V_{C_1} + V_f$, where V_{C_1} is the voltage across ramp capacitor C_1 and after buffering becomes one of the inputs to A_3. The combination of all inputs to

A_3 yields a dc bootstrap circuit with a controlled offset voltage. Thus, current $i_c = (V_{C_1} + V_f - V_{C_1})/R_1 = V_f/R_1$, and the voltage across the capacitor is:

$$V_{C_1} = \int_0^t (i_c/C_1)dt = (V_f/R_1C_1)t$$

C_1 is discharged through transistor Q_1 at time T when V_{C_1} equals the control voltage V_p, which is adjustable from 0 to 2.5 volts. thus $[V_{C1}]_{max} = V_p = (V_f/R_1C_1) T$ and $f = 1/T = V_f/V_pR_1C_1$. The 311 comparator has a trigger output to synchronize external circuitry for easy operation.

The slope of the control voltage versus frequency in kilohertz is 1 for $1 < V_f < 10$ volts. This linear relationship holds even for slow ramps (increasing the value of C_1) with small values of V_f. Capacitor C_2 is selected to maintain the 311's output in a high state long enough so that C_1 may be completely discharged through Q_1 during the appropriate portion of the cycle. □

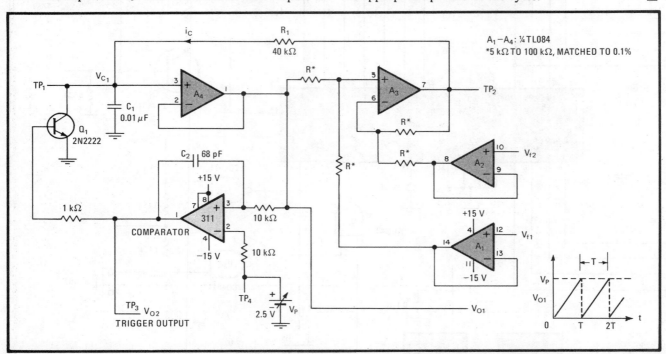

Potentially proportioned. A two-chip, one-transistor ramp generator is linearly adjusted by two dc control signals; with V_p setting the amplitude from 0 to 2.5 volts and V_f and V_p setting the frequency over the range of 0 to 10 kilohertz. Proportional control is achieved by placing ramp capacitor C_1 in the dc bootstrap circuit of A_3 and A_4, which ensures that constant current i_c is a function of only V_f and R_1.

Interleaving decoder simplifies serial-to-parallel conversion

by A. J. Bryant
Manelco Electronics Ltd., Winnipeg, Manitoba, Canada

Four low-cost chips combine to convert a 6-bit serial pulse train into its parallel equivalent in this decoder. Its circuitry is simplified because the bits are broken into two data streams so that it takes only two 4-bit shift registers and a latch to do the conversion.

A synchronous pulse (derived from a pulse detector that is not shown in the figure) is applied to flip-flops A and D ($\frac{1}{2}$74C73), initiating the conversion. The serial stream of negative-going pulses that will be decoded is also applied to flip-flop A, which serves as a divide-by-2 counter.

Both outputs of flip-flop A are then applied to two 4-bit shift registers (4015)—one through one-shot B, which serves as a clock for stepping the corresponding complementary signal of A to register L, and the other through one-shot C, which performs the same function of loading data into shift register H. As seen from the timing diagram, this asynchronous loading arrangement permits the 6-bit input stream to be split and then interlaced, with shift register L receiving low-order bits b_1 to b_4, and shift register H taking bits b_5 to b_6.

All 6 bits are then positioned onto the lines of the 74C174 6-bit latch and strobed onto the latch by one-shot D on the next recurring synchronous pulse. The pulse width of D must be thinner than the synchronous pulse so that its use as the data-valid output does not overlap a new frame. □

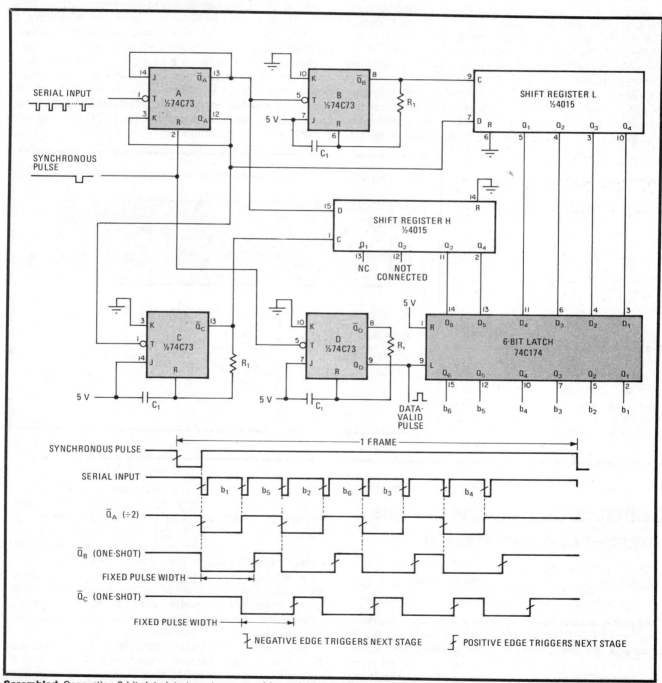

Scrambled. Separating 6-bit data into two streams enables serial-to-parallel conversion with only four chips. The timing diagram clarifies the bit-interleaving method used and details circuit operation. Timing components R_1 and C_1 for one-shots B and C should be selected to ensure that their on-time exceeds two data bits; R_t and C_t should be chosen to ensure there is no overlap with synchronous pulse into a new frame.

Analog multiplexer and op amp unite for precise d-a converter

by Dil Sukh Jain
National Remote Sensing Agency, Hyderabad, India

This simple low-cost digital-to-analog converter uses just an operational amplifier and an analog multiplexer to convert a 4-bit digital input into an analog output. Cascading an additional 16-channel analog multiplexer will extend the input digital word length of the d-a converter to 8 bits. The accuracy and the stability of the converter depend mainly on the accuracy of the resistors and stability of the reference voltage.

Operational amplifier U_1 operates as an inverting amplifier with a weighted-resistor switching network connected in its feedback path. The 16-channel analog multiplexer, U_2, functions as the resistor switching network that is controlled by the four binary inputs A_0–A_3. A 4-bit input, whose decimal equivalent is N, switches multiplexer channel $Y_n - Z$ on and provides a feedback resistance of $R_f = NR$. Thus U_2 sets as the gain of the amplifier a value that corresponds to the equivalent digital input.

The analog output of the d-a converter is $V_O = -(R_f/R_i)V_R = -(NR/R)V_R = -NV_R$, where V_R is a stable reference voltage used in the circuit. The above relationship shows that the analog output V_O is proportional by a factor of V_R to the digital input:

As an example, consider a 4-bit input 0101, whose decimal equivalent is N = 5. Using, for simplicity, a reference voltage of $V_R = -1$ volt, the circuit produces an analog output of $V_O = -5(-1)v = +5$ v.

Op amp NE531 offers a high slew rate for high-speed operation. The circuit may be used as a programmable-gain-control amplifier whose desired gain can be set by thumbwheel switches. In addition, by interchanging input resistor R and multiplexer U_2, the circuit can serve as a programmable attenuator. □

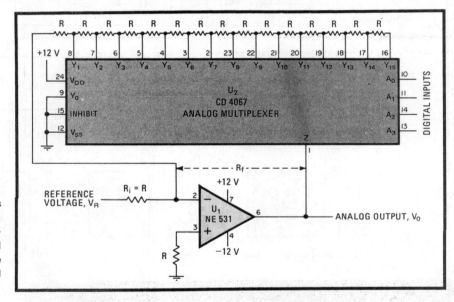

D-a converter. Analog multiplexer U_2 places resistors in the feedback path of amplifier U_1 to control the latter's gain and thereby produce an output proportional to the digital input. The analog output $V_O = -NV_R$, where N is the decimal equivalent of the digital input and V_R is the reference voltage.

Switched-capacitor technique improves a-d conversion

by M. Lobjinski and R. Bermbach
Technical University of Darmstadt, Darmstadt, West Germany

For the precise measurement of dc voltages there already exist many integrating converters. All use a resistor to transform the input voltage into a current that is integrated and then compensated through a switched reference source. This analog-to-digital converter eliminates component influence by using the switched-capacitor technique. It can determine an analog voltage with a maximum error of 2 millivolts.

The charge-balancing a-d converter (Fig. 1a) uses a complementary-MOS D-type flip-flop that functions as a comparator, a latch, and a switch. The input voltage V_{in} is integrated by U_1 and, depending on whether the integrator output voltage is higher or lower than the C-MOS threshold voltage, the clock latches a logic 1 or 0 in the flip-flop. The counter, together with the simple gate, counts the compensation pulses and determines the input voltage. The compensation of the input voltage V_{in} is made by balancing the charge in the integrating capacitor C_1.

Unfortunately the output resistance of flip-flop U_2 depends on its logic state, so that resistor R_2 must have a value much higher than 1 kilohm to cancel the error due to varying output resistance. As a result, two extremely well-matched megohm resistors are needed—a problem that is solved by the switched-capacitor technique (Fig.

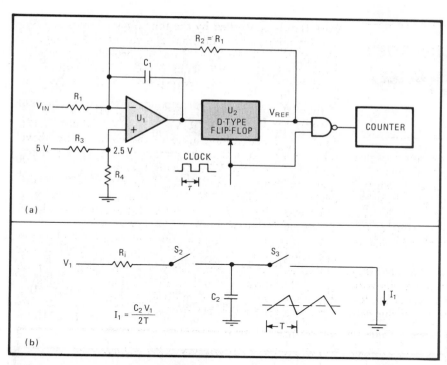

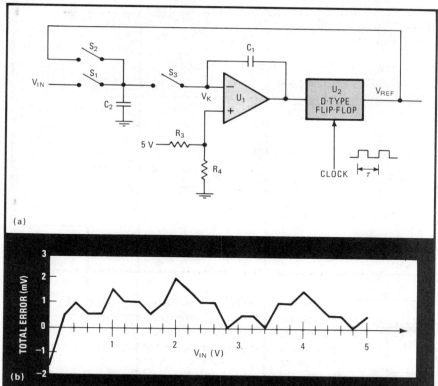

1b), which replaces each resistor with two switches and a capacitor. As shown in the figure, switches S_2 and S_3 are closed successively to charge and discharge, respectively, capacitor C_2 with current $I_1 = C_2V_1/2t$, where t is the total charge and discharge time of C_2 and is greater than $10R_iC_2$. The above relationship shows that the current is independent of R_i.

Incorporating this technique, the converter is modified (Fig. 2a) as a precise a-d converter. The input voltage for 5,000 clock pulses is given by $V_{in} = (N_o + 5,000 - 2N_k)$ millivolts, where N_o is the number of cycles in which the flip-flop output is at ground and N_k is total offset voltage. The plot of error versus the input voltage given in Fig. 2b shows that the maximum error is 2 mv. □

A-d converter linearizes 100-ohm temperature detector

by Anthony Parise
Neutronics Inc., King of Prussia, Pa.

Conventional methods of linearizing resistance temperature detectors use a diode-resistor ladder circuit but do not produce a true straight line. However, this circuit (see figure) linearizes a 100-ohm platinum resistance temperature detector and uses few parts. With an analog-to-digital converter, such as ICL7106, a digital thermometer can easily be built.

For this detector, temperature is:

$$T = \frac{1,000(R_T - k_0)}{k_2 - k_1(R_T - k_0)}$$

where R_T is the resistance of the detector in ohms at temperature T and k_0, k_1, and k_2 are constants that are listed in the figure. Current I develops a voltage across R_0 that compensates for the 0° reading (in either Celsius or Fahrenheit) and the detector's lead resistance by raising input low V_0 volts above reference point A.

The input to the converter is now $V_{input} = V_T - V_0$. Voltage V_2, across R_2, corresponds to reference constant k_2, and the ratio R_a/R_b is selected so that it equals k_1. As a result, U_1's reference input voltage $= V_2 - k_1 V_{input} = V_2 - k_1(V_T - V_0)$.

The value displayed with the 7106 is equal to 1,000 $(V_{input}/V_{reference})$. Substituting for V_{input} and $V_{reference}$, the equation for display reduces to:

$$\frac{1,000 I(R_T - R_0)}{I R_2 - k_1 I(R_T - R_0)}$$

The expression for T may be reduced by canceling I in the equation and substituting k_0 for R_0 and k_2 for R_2. R_0 and R_2 must be temperature-stable and adjustable to provide easy calibration and have similar temperature coefficients. If a binary output is needed for a microprocessor interface, 12-bit binary a-d converter ICL7109 is recommended for U_1. □

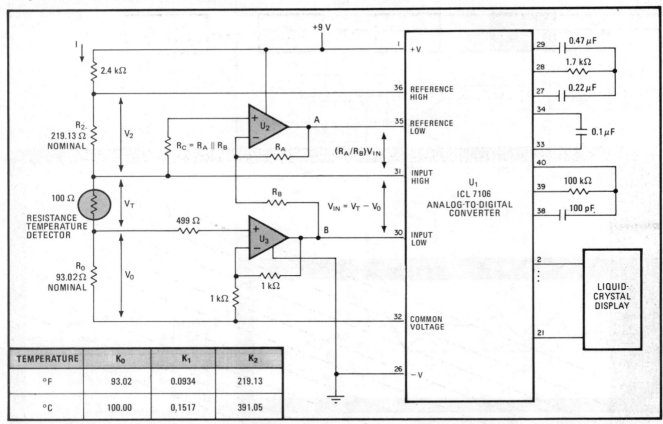

TEMPERATURE	K_0	K_1	K_2
°F	93.02	0.0934	219.13
°C	100.00	0.1517	391.05

Linearize. The general linear equation relating resistance to temperature is implemented with two op amps and a-d converter ICL7106. The display corresponds to an output given by 1,000 $(V_{input}/V_{reference})$, which when simplified is identical to the equation for temperature T.

FILTERS

Selecting the right filters for digital phase detectors

by Charles R. Jackson
E-Systems Inc., St. Petersburg, Fla.

Digital phase detectors are widely used in phase-locked loops because of their inherent high speed, large frequency coverage, and simplicity of operation. However, such detectors generate spurious alternating-current components that degrade the loop's performance. This design technique analyzes these spurious sidebands, enabling the designer to quickly project the performance of a PLL as a function of the frequency divider, the reference frequency, and the desired loop bandwidth. As a result, the proper filter for the circuit is precisely selected.

A single-loop frequency synthesizer (a) may be used to analyze the detector's spurious output. Spurious sidebands generated with the detector are minimized when a narrow bandwidth is set. As a result, phase tracking is degraded and lock-up slowed. A general expression for these spurious sidebands is S/C (sideband-to-carrier ratio) = $20 \log (\Delta f/2f)$, where Δf = voltage-controlled–oscillator peak deviation and f = modulation rate. Simplifying the above expression in terms of the loop bandwidth (B), the numeric value of the frequency divider in the PLL feedback loop (N), and the reference frequency f_r, S/C = $20 \log(4BN/2f_r)$. This equation was developed using no low-pass filter in the generalized PLL and setting $f = f_r$.

On the plot of S/C in decibels versus the loop band-

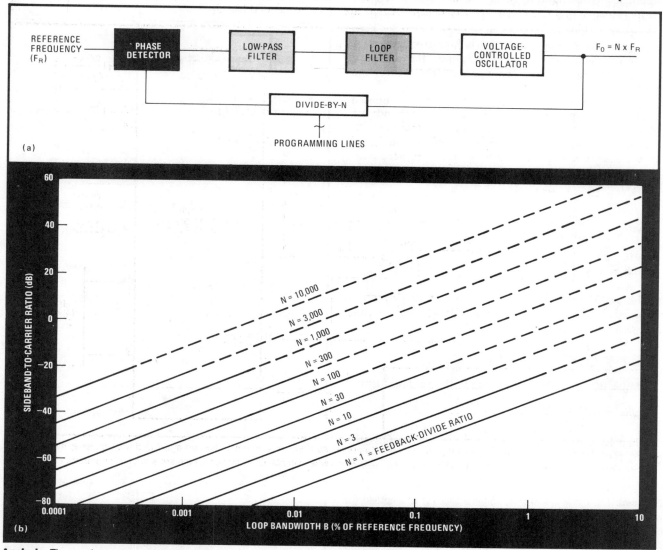

Analysis. The spurious output of a digital detector (a) is analyzed and an expression is developed for the sideband-to-carrier ratio. S/C in decibels is plotted versus loop bandwidth, which is expressed as a percentage of the loop reference frequency for various values of N.

width for various values of N (b), B is expressed as a percentage of the loop reference frequency. In addition, the dotted lines are extensions of the equation for $\Delta f/f$ greater than 0.2.

For example, to find the loop bandwidth for S/C = −50 dB with the VCO operating at 3 megahertz and the reference frequency at 100 kilohertz, N must first be calculated. In this case it is equal to the $(3\times10^6)/(100\times10^3)$, or 30. The intersection of the −50-dB line and N = 30 (see b) gives a value of 0.0053% (f_r) for B. Hence the actual value of B = 5.3 hertz, or $5.3\times10^{-5}\times100\times10^3$. However, if the loop bandwidth is increased to 500 Hz, a low-pass filter is needed to maintain a −50-dB value for S/C.

To determine the low-pass filter's characteristics, a new value of B must be calculated that is equal to 0.5%. The intersection of 0.5% and N = 30 gives S/C = −10 dB. Thus the low-pass filter needs to provide −40 dB. □

State-variable filter trims predecessor's component count

by James H. Hahn
Interface Technology Inc., St. Louis, Mo.

A state-variable active filter, even though it requires three operational amplifiers and eight passive components, is widely used because it is less sensitive than other filter designs to component changes, provides high Q and gain, and can operate at fairly high frequencies. A new design using fewer parts simplifies the standard filter[1] yet provides the same bandpass characteristics and low sensitivity.

A conventional state-variable circuit (a) is composed of summing amplifier A_1 and integrators A_2 and A_3. When high-pass output E_2 is eliminated and the first integrator is treated as the summing amplifier, the bandpass transfer function of the revised circuit (b) becomes:

$$H_{bp}(s) = \frac{E_3}{E_1} = \frac{-s/C_1R_1}{s^2 + sa + b}$$

where $a = \dfrac{R_2C_2(R_3+R_4)+R_4C_1R_5}{R_2R_5C_1C_2(R_3+R_4)}$

and $b = \dfrac{R_4(R_1+R_5)}{C_1C_2R_1R_2R_5(R_3+R_4)}$

In addition, the two-pole bandpass form of the circuit is preserved. If R_5 is eliminated and left an open circuit, the a and b terms simplify to:

$a = \dfrac{R_4}{C_2R_2(R_3+R_4)}$ and $b = \dfrac{R_4}{C_1C_2R_1R_2(R_3+R_4)}$

Comparing the transfer function to the general form:

$$H_{bp} = \frac{s\omega_0H_0/Q}{s^2 + s(\omega_0/Q) + \omega_0^2}$$

When H_0 is the value of H_{bp} at $\omega = \omega_0$ and Q is the quality factor:

Reduced. The conventional state-variable filter (a) is simplified (b) when highpass output E_2 is eliminated and integrator A_2 is treated as a summing amplifier. This circuit is further reduced by creating an open circuit across R_5. A reduced two-pole bandpass state-variable filter for f_0 = 941 Hz, Q = 15, and R_3/R_4 = 1 is shown in (c). A version with R_4 and R_5 open and R_3 = 0 is shown in (d).

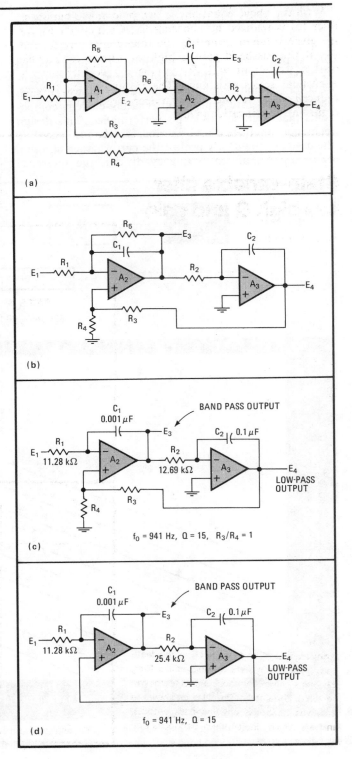

(a)

(b)

(c) f_0 = 941 Hz, Q = 15, R_3/R_4 = 1

(d) f_0 = 941 Hz, Q = 15

$$\omega_o = \left[\frac{R_4}{C_1C_2R_1R_2(R_3+R_4)}\right]^{1/2}$$

$$\text{and } H_o = -Q^2 = \frac{-C_2R_2(R_3+R_4)}{C_1R_1R_4}$$

Solving for R_1 and R_2:

$$R_1 = \frac{1}{\omega_oQC_1} \text{ and } R_2 = \frac{R_4Q}{(R_3+R_4)\omega_oC_2}$$

With the above equations, a two-pole active bandpass filter (c) is realized by choosing C_1, C_2, and $R_3:R_4$ for the given value of ω_o and Q and then computing R_1 and R_2. If the passband gain is high, an attenuator can be used at the input with R_1 serving as the attenuator's equivalent series resistance. The circuit can be further reduced (d) by letting R_4 be an open circuit and $R_3 = 0$ ohm. This modification gives:

$$\omega_o{}^2 = \frac{1}{C_1C_2R_1R_2} \text{ where}$$

$$R_1 = \frac{1}{\omega_oQC_1} \text{ and } R_2 = \frac{Q}{\omega_oC_2}$$

The simplified configuration uses much less power and fewer components than the conventional circuit to achieve the same low sensitivities. If C_2 is greater than C_1, the circuit's near ideal performance will not be degraded by second-order effects, such as finite amplifier gain. The filter is also useful for low-pass applications. □

References
1. J. Graeme, G. E. Tobey, and L. P. Huelsman, "Operational Amplifiers—Design and Applications," McGraw-Hill, 1971, p. 304.

State-variable filter has high Q and gain

by Kamil Kraus
Rokycany, Czechoslovakia

Although much work has been done in developing state-variable filters that use three or two operational amplifiers, earlier designs [*Electronics*, April 21, 1982, p. 126] suffer from a common disadvantage in that the filter's

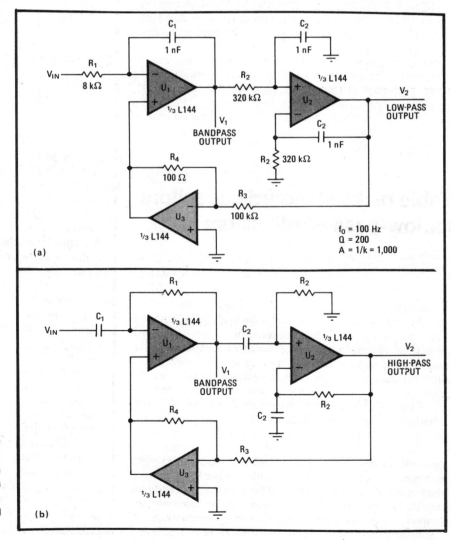

Independent. With inverter U_3 in the feedback loop of the state-variable active filter, the filter's center frequency and Q factor can be tuned separately. The filter as shown in (a) gives bandpass and low-pass outputs, and the version in (b) gives bandpass and high-pass outputs.

center frequency and the Q factor are interdependent. This new design provides a solution by introducing a parameter k in the transfer function of the filter.

The circuit uses three op amps, U_1 through U_3, to realize the filter. U_1 and U_2 function as negative and positive integrators, and U_3 completes the feedback loop. The second-order state-variable filter in (a) provides a bandpass output V_1 and a low-pass output V_2. Its transfer function is $V_1/V_{in} = -Qs/(1+s/Q+s^2)$ and $V_2/V_{in} = -1/k(1+s/Q+s^2)$ where $s = j\omega/\omega_0$, $1/\omega_0^2 = C_1C_2R_1R_2/k$, $Q = (C_2R_2/kC_1R_1)^{1/2}$, and $k = R_4/R_3$. The parameter ω_0 is the center frequency of the filter. Using $C_1 = C_2 = C$ in the above equations, $R_1 = 1/CQ\omega_0$ and $R_2 = kQ/C\omega_0$.

The filter in (b) gives a bandpass output V_1 and a high-pass output V_2. As a result, its transfer function can be written as $V_1/V_{in} = -Qs/(1+s/Q+s^2)$ and $V_2/V_{in} = -(s^2k)/(1+s/Q+s^2)$ where $1/\omega_0^2 = kC_1C_2R_1R_2$ and $Q = (C_1R_1/kC_2R_2)^{1/2}$. Letting $C_1 = C_2 = C$ yields $R_1 = Q/\omega_0C$ and $R_2 = 1/\omega_0kQC$.

As an illustration, the filter in (a) is realized for a Q factor of 200 and a center frequency of 100 hertz. The design assumes a value of 1 nanofarad for C_1 and C_2. With the equations shown above, the values obtained are $R_1 = 8$ kilohms, $R_2 = 320$ kΩ, $R_4 = 100$ Ω, and $R_3 = 100$ kΩ. The gain provided by the filter is $A = 1/k = 1,000$. The circuit uses components with 1% tolerances to reduce frequency drift and enhance circuit reliability. □

Table picks standard capacitors for low-pass elliptic filters

by Edward E. Wetherhold
Honeywell Inc., Signal Analysis Center, Annapolis, Md.

An equally terminated elliptic-function low-pass filter may be fabricated with this design aid. The circuit's three nonresonating shunt capacitors have standard capacitive values, while the resonating condensers use nonstandard values because they tune the inductors to infinite frequencies. The elliptic-design method is applicable to all fifth-degree elliptic low-pass filters, regardless of cut-off frequency or impedance level.

Although the design table is based on the circuit having equal impedance terminations of 500 ohms, other impedance levels may be scaled while maintaining the standard values for C_1, C_3, and C_5 (see table). For example, to scale the design table higher or lower in frequency by a factor of 10 or 100, multiply or divide all frequencies by 10 or 100 and divide or multiply all components values by the same factor, respectively.

Similarly, to scale the designs to impedance levels other than 500 Ω by, say, a factor of 0.1 or 10, multiply the inductor values and divide the capacitor values of the circuit by the same factor. The frequencies remain unchanged. However, special scaling procedures must be used for impedance values that differ from 500 Ω and are not factors of 10.

A simple example illustrates the use of the table for an impedance factor equal to a nonintegral power of 10. Consider the case of a filter whose 3-decibel cutoff frequency, f_3^x, is 100 kilohertz and the terminating impedance is 600 Ω. The designer must:

■ Calculate the scaled impedance factor through the equation $R = Z_x/500$.
■ Calculate the 3-dB cutoff frequency of a 500-Ω filter from $f_3^{500} = R \times f_3^x$.
■ From the table, select the design with the frequency nearest to f_3^{500}. The tabulated values of all capacitors will be used directly in the new design, and the inductor values will be scaled.
■ Calculate the exact value of $f_3^x = f^{1\,500}_3/R$, where $f^{1\,500}_3$ is the tabulated 3-dB frequency. In a similar manner, determine all other frequencies.
■ Calculate the new inductance values for the desired terminating impedance from $L = R^2 \times L_{500}$.

Given that $Z_x = 600$ Ω and $f_3^x = 100$ kHz, $R = 600/500 = 1.2$, $R^2 = 1.44$, and $f_3^{500} = 1.2(100)$kHz = 120 kHz, filter No. 2 is selected from the table because

LOW-PASS ELLIPTIC FILTERS FOR 500-Ω TERMINATIONS

Filter No.	Frequency (kHz)			Stopband attenuation (dB)	Reflection coefficient (%)	Capacitors (pF)					Inductors (μH)		Frequency (kHz)	
	F_{CO}	F_3	F_{A_s}			C_1	C_3	C_5	C_2	C_4	L_2	L_4	F_2	F_4
1	79.5	98.9	157	47.4	4.40	2,700	5,600	2,200	324	937	1,207	1,009	254	164
2	106	120	177	46.2	10.5	2,700	4,700	2,200	341	982	936	756	282	185
3	147	157	215	45.4	22.7	2,700	3,900	2,200	364	1,045	632	488	332	223
4	92.9	118	191	48.0	3.71	2,200	4,700	1,800	257	743	1,018	859	311	199
5	127	145	217	46.7	9.69	2,200	3,900	1,800	271	779	785	639	345	226
6	169	182	254	45.9	19.7	2,200	3,300	1,800	287	821	564	442	396	264
7	112	144	241	49.8	3.42	1,800	3,900	1,500	192	549	845	725	395	252
8	149	173	270	48.8	8.40	1,800	3,300	1,500	200	570	675	562	433	281
9	211	227	327	47.8	20.2	1,800	2,700	1,500	213	604	455	364	512	340
10	128	166	263	46.3	3.11	1,500	3,300	1,200	192	561	720	600	428	274
11	179	206	299	44.8	8.89	1,500	2,700	1,200	204	592	552	442	475	311
12	252	270	363	43.8	20.8	1,500	2,200	1,200	220	636	371	282	558	376
13	156	208	355	50.1	2.69	1,200	2,700	1,000	127	363	588	507	583	371
14	223	259	404	48.8	8.40	1,200	2,200	1,000	133	380	450	375	650	422
15	317	341	490	47.8	20.2	1,200	1,800	1,000	142	402	303	242	768	510
16	194	252	415	48.4	3.11	1,000	2,200	820	115	331	479	406	678	434
17	273	314	473	47.0	9.05	1,000	1,800	820	121	348	366	299	756	493
18	373	402	563	46.2	19.7	1,000	1,500	820	129	368	256	201	876	585
19	239	311	520	49.4	3.15	820	1,800	680	89.3	256	391	335	851	544
20	326	379	585	48.2	8.46	820	1,500	680	93.6	267	307	254	939	610
21	483	517	730	47.2	22.1	820	1,200	680	100	286	195	154	1,136	758
22	285	371	615	48.8	3.06	680	1,500	560	76.6	220	326	278	1,007	643
23	416	474	714	47.3	9.95	680	1,200	560	81.3	233	240	197	1,139	744
24	572	613	858	46.5	21.5	680	1,000	560	86.3	246	165	130	1,333	891
25	367	469	795	50.5	3.66	560	1,200	470	57.6	164	259	223	1,302	831
26	502	577	901	49.4	9.57	560	1,000	470	60.3	171	201	168	1,447	940
27	718	768	1,106	48.6	22.5	560	820	470	64.1	181	132	106	1,730	1,150
28	440	560	924	49.3	3.81	470	1,000	390	51.4	147	216	184	1,510	966
29	617	701	1,063	48.0	10.5	470	820	390	54.2	155	163	134	1,696	1,107
30	863	920	1,295	47.3	23.2	470	680	390	57.6	164	109	85.7	2,013	1,344
31	547	691	1,179	51.3	4.11	390	820	330	38.5	109	176	152	1,930	1,233
32	755	859	1,351	50.2	10.8	390	680	330	40.4	114	134	112	2,166	1,408
33	1,086	1,155	1,675	49.5	24.8	390	560	330	42.8	120	86.2	69.5	2,620	1,741
34	659	817	1,299	47.7	4.57	330	680	270	39.0	112	146	122	2,109	1,357
35	910	1,021	1,498	46.5	11.8	330	560	270	41.2	118	109	88.1	2,372	1,559
36	1,244	1,321	1,809	45.8	24.1	330	470	270	43.9	125	74.1	57.3	2,792	1,877

its f_3^{500} value is closest to 120 kHz. Thus C_1 = 2,700 picofarads, C_3 = 4,700 pF, C_5 = 2,200 pF, C_2 = 341 pF, and C_4 = 982 pF. Inductors L_2 = 1.44(936) = 1,348 microhenrys and L_4 = 1.44(756) = 1,089 μH. Note that design No. 2 has a reflection coefficient of 10.5%. If a lower voltage standing-wave ratio is desired, then design No. 4, which has a reflection coefficient of 3.71%, must be incorporated. Only 10% capacitor values are used in the table. Those interested in obtaining 5% designs may circle 270 on the reader service card. □

Delay line eases comb-filter design

by Hanan Kupferman
Century Data Systems Inc., Anaheim, Calif.

Designing a multiple-frequency notch filter with standard band-stop transfer functions is complicated and tedious because the process needs repeating. In addition, filter matching is difficult for sections with different band-stop frequencies. Through exploiting the characteristics of a delay line, this comb filter is easily realized and provides a band-stop response for a fundamental frequency and its harmonics. The fundamental frequency corresponds to the delay time of the delay line.

The general scheme of the filter (a) shows that the delay line with a delay τ and characteristic impedance R is driven by and equals matched impedance sources R_1 and R_2. Use of input and output buffers in the circuit is optional. The fundamental frequency where the first notch occurs is $f_1 = 1/\tau$. Other band stops occur at $f_2 = 2/\tau$, $f_3 = 3/\tau$, and so on. Related to the rise time of the delay line, the filter's bandwidth determines how many harmonic frequencies will be attenuated. If the rise time of the line is faster, the bandwidth is wider, and therefore the stop-band range is higher.

This comb filter (b) is designed for a fundamental notch frequency of 961 kilohertz. The delay time of the delay line is 1,040 nanoseconds. Transistors Q_1 and Q_2 serve as input buffers, with Q_3 and Q_4 serving as output buffers. A degradation occurs in the attenuation of high-

Combing. The general scheme (a) of the comb filter utilizes a delay line to stop the fundamental frequency and its harmonics. The fundamental frequency $f_1 = 1/\tau$, where τ is the delay provided by the line. The characteristic impedance of the line is equal to source impedances R_1 and R_2. A comb filter (b) uses a 1,040-nanosecond delay line to obtain a notch at 961 kHz and its harmonics (c).

er harmonics (c) and can be attributed to the rise time of the delay line. The magnitude of stop-band attenuation at higher frequencies can be improved by using a delay line with a faster rise time. □

Sample-and-hold devices ease tracking-filter design

by Ralph J. Amodeo and Gerald T. Volpe
University of Bridgeport, Bridgeport, Conn.

Tracking filters are often required for either passing or rejecting a carrier signal that varies over a certain frequency range. This design presents an active sample-and-hold resistor-capacitor filter that tracks an input carrier's frequency by using its own notch frequency. The circuit uses sample-and-hold devices, operational amplifiers, and RC elements. In addition, the filter is insensitive to component changes and uses equal-valued capacitors, which makes it attractive for monolithic integrated-circuit implementation.

This biquadratic filter (a) uses zero-order-hold ICs ZOH_2 and ZOH_3 to perform unit-delay function z^{-1}, where z is the Z-transform variable; ZOH_1 and ZOH_4 are used for data buffering. To obtain a second-order delay, ZOH_3 is strobed before ZOH_2 to ensure that the data at reference point N_2 is properly transferred to N_1 before N_2 is updated.

Also, ZOH_1 prevents the input voltage to ZOH_2 from changing until ZOH_1 is strobed. Without this feature, ZOH_2's output can modify its own input voltage, thus causing erroneous data transfer.

The timing generator (b) provides strobe pulses for the filter and operates at a sampling frequency that is 16 times the filter-notch frequency, f_o. The Harris 2820PLL and divider U_1 generates the clock frequency. Divider U_2 and shift register U_3 provide the four-phase strobe pulses.

Analysis of the filter yields a biquadratic Z-transformed transfer function:

$$H(z) = \frac{H_o(ez^2 - cz + d)}{z^2 - az + b}, \text{ where } H_o = \alpha\beta$$

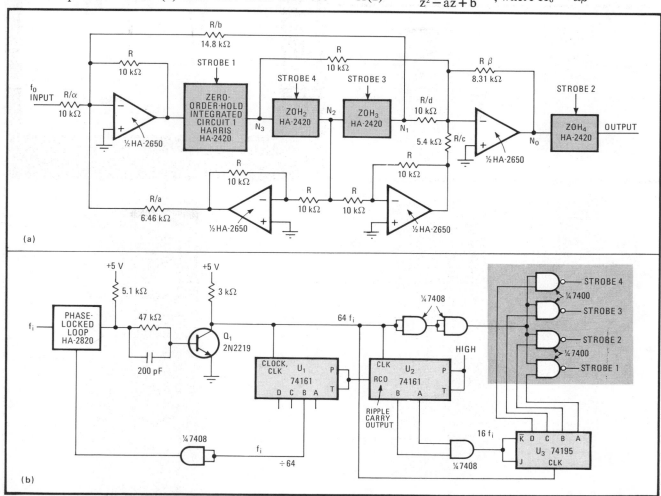

Tracking. The notch frequency of this tracking filter tracks the input carrier frequency and provides modulation information. The band-reject filter (a) is designed for a notch frequency of 13.5 kHz, Q = 1, and ξ = 0.5. The zero-order-hold devices provide second-order delays. The timing generator (b) provides strobe pulses for the filter.

Parameters a, b, c, and d control the filter's natural frequency, quality factor, notch frequency, and notch depth, respectively. In addition, parameter e is a constant, α is the filter's amplification factor, and β is the feedback factor.

The filter's gain (H_o) is controlled by input summing resistor R/α and feedback resistor $R\beta$. In order to obtain a notch-frequency response, $a = 2e^{-\xi\omega_o\tau} \cos(\omega_o\tau [1-\xi^2]^{1/2})$, $b = e^{-2\xi\omega_o\tau}$, $c = 2\cos\omega_o\tau$, $d = 1$, and $e = 1$, where ξ is a frequency constant.

With a sampling frequency of $16f_o$, $\omega_o\tau = \pi/8$. Therefore, as τ increases, ω_o decreases in order to maintain the value of $\omega_o\tau$. As an example, a second-order band-reject filter is designed with its notch frequency at 13.5 kilohertz, $Q = 1$, and $\xi = 0.5$. Substituting the data into the transfer equation yields:

$$H(z) = \frac{H_o(z^2 - 1.848z + 1)}{z^2 - 1.549z + 0.6752}$$

At dc ($z = 1$) the transfer-function factor is $H(1) = 1.204H_o$. For this equation, a scale factor of $H_o = 1/1.204 = 0.8306$ is used. This factor reduces the equation by 0.8306. The reciprocals of a, b, c, and d are the fixed resistor values that are scaled by a convenient constant R. The practical resistor values obtained are as shown in the figure. □

FREQUENCY MULTIPLIERS

Joining a PLL and VCO forms fractional frequency multiplier

by S. K. Seth, S. K. Roy, R. Dattagupta, and D. K. Basu
Jadavpur University, Calcutta, India

Most frequency multipliers are hampered by the fact that they can multiply frequencies only in integer amounts. As a result, if a certain output frequency is desired, the input frequency must be carefully selected. Such exact choosing is no longer needed because this circuit can multiply pulse frequencies by any real number through the simple adjustment of two potentiometers. In addition, it operates over a wide input-frequency range and has a more stable output than do conventional multipliers.

This design combines a phase-locked–loop frequency-to-voltage converter and an external voltage-controlled oscillator for pulse-frequency multiplication. However, conventional multiplication circuits employing PLLs use either harmonic locking or a frequency divider between its VCO and phase comparator. Thus, the output is only an integer multiple of the input.

A PLL connected as a frequency demodulator, generates voltage V_d that is related to the input frequency by

$V_d = kf_{in}$, where k is a constant and f_{in} is the frequency of the input signal. In addition, the input frequency of the internal VCO (contained in the PLL) is $f_{in} = V_d/VR_1C_1$, where R_1 and C_1 are the frequency-determining components of the internal VCO and V is the supply voltage.

Demodulated voltage V_d is fed to the control-voltage input of the external VCO whose output frequency is $f_{out} = V_d/VR_2C_2$, where R_2 and C_2 are frequency-determining components of the external VCO. Solving for the output frequency: $f_{out} = f_{in}R_1C_1/R_2C_2$ and thus $n = (R_1C_1)/(R_2C_2)$. The multiplication factor n is only determined by the externally connected resistors and capacitors and therefore can be chosen for any value.

The circuit (a) uses National Semiconductor's general-purpose PLL LM565 and VCO LM566. Operational amplifier μA741 serves as the buffer between the two.

The multiplication factor for this particular circuit is 6.15, and its input-frequency range is 2 to 6 kilohertz. The oscilloscope display (b) shows the input and output waveforms for an input frequency of 4 kHz and multiplication factor of 6.15. For stable circuit operation, R_1 and C_1 should be selected according to the input frequency, and R_2 and C_2 should be chosen to generate the desired multiplication factor. □

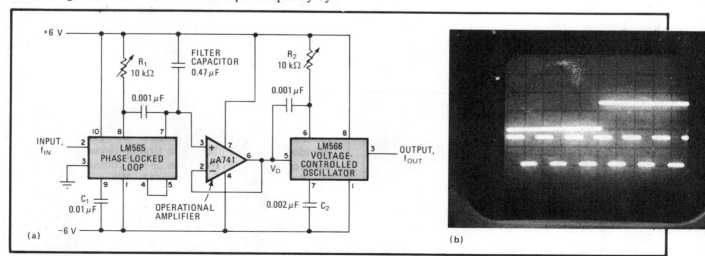

Multiplier. The circuit (a) uses a phase-locked loop, an external voltage-controlled oscillator, and a buffer. The oscilloscope display (b) shows the input and output waveform for an input frequency of 4 kHz and a multiplication factor of 6.15.

Phase shifters simplify
frequency-multiplier design

by Fred Brown
Lake San Marcos, Calif.

Phase-shift frequency multipliers, unlike conventional multipliers, can produce a spectrally pure output without filtering. However, by using wideband phase-difference networks for phase splitting, frequency-independent multipliers over many octaves may be obtained.

The principle of this type of multiplier is shown in Fig.1a. A sine-wave frequency is multiplied N times by dividing the input into N different phases that are equal-

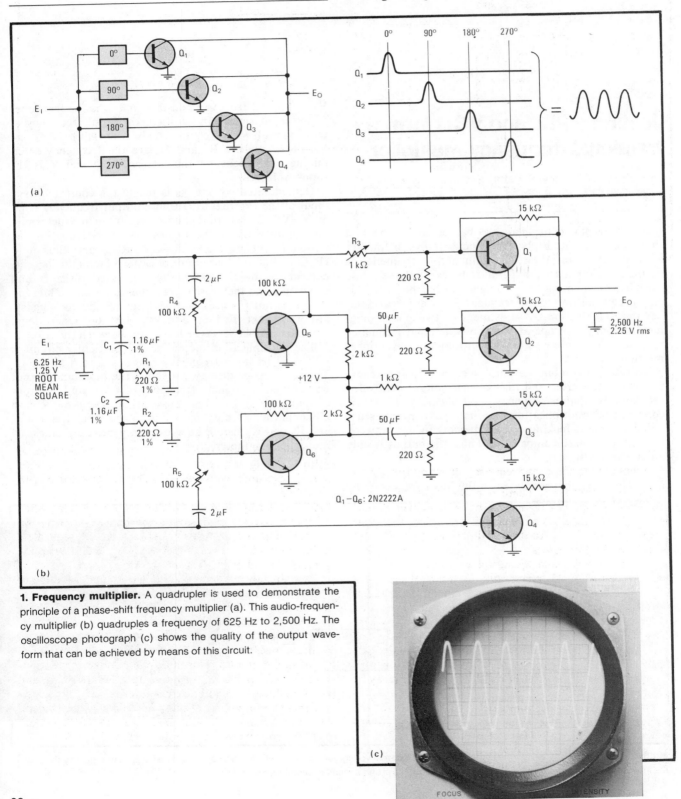

1. Frequency multiplier. A quadrupler is used to demonstrate the principle of a phase-shift frequency multiplier (a). This audio-frequency multiplier (b) quadruples a frequency of 625 Hz to 2,500 Hz. The oscilloscope photograph (c) shows the quality of the output waveform that can be achieved by means of this circuit.

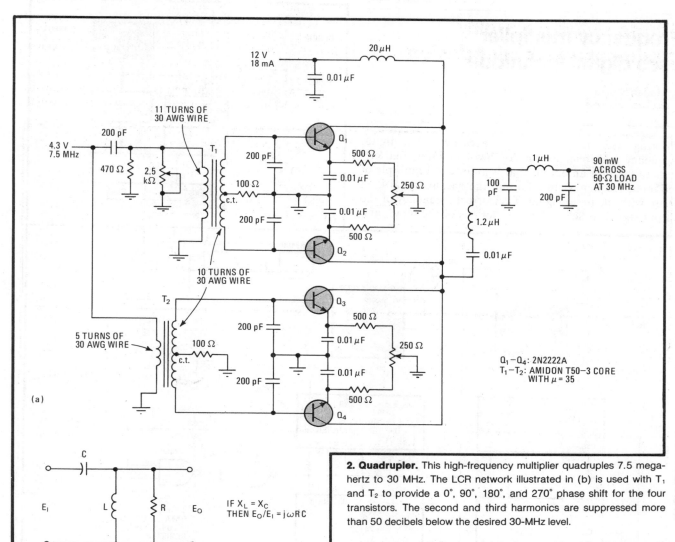

2. Quadrupler. This high-frequency multiplier quadruples 7.5 megahertz to 30 MHz. The LCR network illustrated in (b) is used with T_1 and T_2 to provide a 0°, 90°, 180°, and 270° phase shift for the four transistors. The second and third harmonics are suppressed more than 50 decibels below the desired 30-MHz level.

ly spaced through 360°. These N phases drive N class-C transistors whose outputs are combined to deliver a pulse every 360°/N. The use of N transistors allows the input power to the circuit to be N times as high without saturating the transistors.

This audio-frequency quadrupler (Fig.1b) uses frequency-dependent 90° phase-shift networks R_1 C_1, and R_2, C_2. Transistors Q_1 and Q_4 provide pulses that are shifted 0° and 90° in phase at the output. Phase inversion of the pulses is achieved by transistors Q_5 and Q_6, which drive Q_2 and Q_3 to provide pulses that are 180°- and 270°-phase-shifted at the output. The output pulses that are 90° apart are combined to produce the quadrupled frequency. The af multiplier quadruples a frequency of 625 hertz to 2,500 Hz.

The amplitude of the input signal is adjusted for the proper level at the base of Q_4. In addition, level adjustments for Q_1, Q_2, and Q_3 are controlled by R_3, R_4, and R_5. The oscilloscope photograph (Fig.1c) shows the quality of the ×4 output frequency at 2,500 Hz.

Phase-shift frequency multipliers are superior to con-

ventional multipliers at high frequencies in subharmonic suppression. A high-frequency version of this type of multiplier (Fig.2a), also a quadrupler, uses a simple LCR phase-shift network (Fig.2b) to produce a 90° phase shift.

An interesting property of this network is that when the reactances are made equal, the phase shift between the input and output ports will always be 90°, regardless of the value of R. This property allows both amplitude (varying R) and phase (varying L or C) control.

The inductance L is created by the primary winding of T_1; the secondary winding delivers a 90° and 270° phase shift to Q_1 and Q_2, respectively. The 0° and 180° phase shifts are provided by T_2 to Q_3 and Q_4.

In addition, the L-pi network at the output provides an optimum match to the 50-ohm load and a little attenuation of subharmonics. This multiplier, unlike conventional ones, is capable of suppressing subharmonics and therefore does not require output filtering.

A spectrum-analyzer display showed that the second and third harmonics could easily be reduced by more than 50 decibels below the desired fourth harmonic. □

Frequency multiplier uses digital technique

by Marian Stofka
Kosice, Czechoslovakia

Offering wide range and high accuracy, this digital frequency multiplier uses a few low-cost integrated circuits to produce an output that is an integral multiple of the input frequency. In addition, the output signal is in phase with the input signal. The correct frequency of the output signals is set within two periods of the input, and

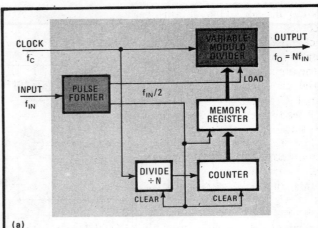

(a)

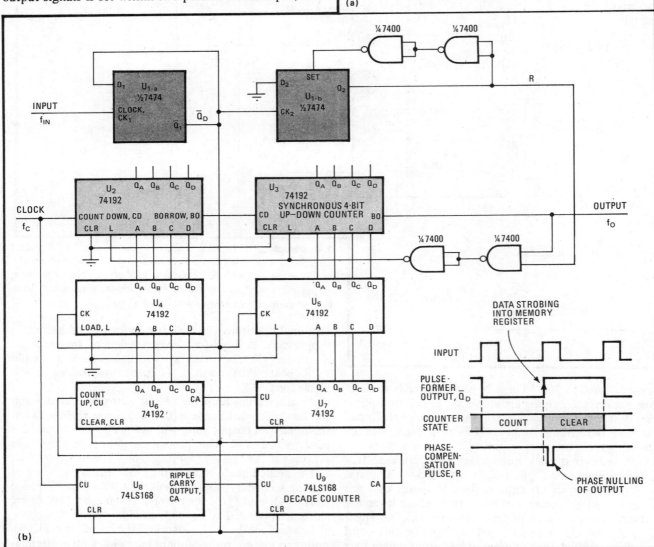

(b)

Multiply by N. The multiplier (a) generates an output whose frequency is N times the frequency of the input signal. The clock is divided by N, and the data is stored in a memory register that determines the modulus of the variable-modulo divider. The output of this divider is given by $f_o = Nf_{in}$. The hardware realization (b) uses a few chips to achieve an output that is 100 times f_{in}.

in fact the design could be integrated into one chip.

The fundamental schematic (a) comprises a pulse-former, divider, counter, memory register, and variable-modulo divider. The clock pulse is divided by N and then counted by the counter for a period corresponding to one cycle of the input signal. At the end of this period the counter output data is strobed into the memory register, which determines the modulus of the variable-modulo divider. This data is valid until new data is accepted. The variable-modulo divider is driven by the clock pulse, and the counter output data at the end of the counting period is $C_o = T_{in}f_c/N$, where T_{in} is the period of the input signal, f_c is the frequency of the clock, and N is the modulus of the divider. As a result, the output signal (f_o) obtained from the variable-modulo divider satisfies the relation $f_o = f_c/C_o = N/T_{in} = Nf_{in}$, where f_o is the frequency of the output signal.

The practical circuit (b) uses two decade counters, six synchronous 4-bit up-down counters, a flip-flop, and a NAND-gate chip to realize the multiplier design. The counter output is stored in the memory register consisting of U_4 and U_5. The clock frequency is determined from the equation $f_c = 0.8N10^k f_{in}$, where k is the number of decade counters connected in the multiplier counter. For the components shown, the output frequency is $f_o = 100f_{in}$. The worst-case relative-output phase error is $10^{-k}/0.6$. The output is compared with the input to ensure the output waveform has the proper phase. □

FUNCTION GENERATORS

Simulating a repeatable pseudorandom pulse train

by Vince Banes
Litton Industries, Amecom division, Melville, N. Y.

A controllable pseudorandom pulse train is often needed to test the ability of a sensor system to detect a noisy repeatable pattern. This pulse-train generator provides up to 16 different pulse intervals with constant widths. Also, the intervals can be altered while the system is running. Integrated circuit 74LS670, a 16-bit TTL random-access memory, is the heart of the design.

The input is a 16-bit word with a strobe command from a computer interface or toggle switches. Data lines WD_0 through WD_{11} are the write-data lines, and WA_0 through WA_3 are the address lines. The data enters the memory when the strobe signal is low. The 1-megahertz clock serves to set the width of the least significant bit to 1 microsecond.

To prevent any changes in pulse pattern, D-type flip-flops U_{4-a} and U_{4-b} shape the output pulses, and 7405 inverters detect the end of a pulse train. The functioning of the circuit may be understood by considering a pattern made of, for example, one 500-μs followed by two 450-μs intervals. This pattern is attained by storing hexadecimal values 1F1, 1BF, and 000 in address lines W_0, WA_1, and WA_2, respectively. Since a zero (000) value is used to mark the end of the data, the minimum pulse interval in this circuit is 3 μs. The generator's output is synchronized by gating the output of the inverters with the synchronizing signal. The gating makes the address counter go back to the beginning of the RAM when a zero data word is detected of a reset needed. □

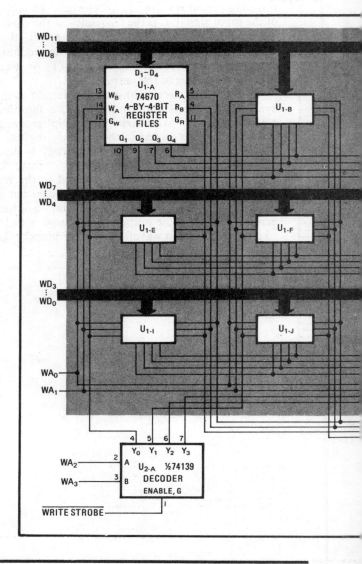

Generator has independent duty cycle and frequency

by Harry H. Lamb
Richmond Hill, Ont., Canada

Using just a 555 timer, two transistors, and an operational-amplifier chip, this pulse generator provides pulses whose duty cycle and frequency of oscillation can be controlled independently. The frequency varies linearly with the gain of the amplifier, and the duty cycle is linearly controlled with a potentiometer.

Transistors Q_1 and Q_2 allow capacitor C to charge only when timer U_2 is not causing it to discharge. As a result, the sum of charge and discharge times remains constant. U_2 switches when the trigger input drops to $V_{cc}/3$ or the threshold input increases to $2V_{cc}/3$. Rearranging the above voltage levels reveals that the threshold-trigger input operates at $V_{cc}(1 \pm 1/3)/2$ and that, as a result, capacitor voltage V_c varies between $V_{cc}(1 + 1/3A)/2$ and $V_{cc}(1 - 1/3A)/2$, where A is the gain of the amplifier U_{1-a} and controls the time required for V_c to take the threshold-trigger input from one switching point to the other. U_{1-b} simply sets the reference $V_{cc}/2$ for U_{1-a}.

During time interval t_{low}, the output of U_2 is low and the capacitor discharges from an initial value of $V_{cc}(1 + 1/3A)/2$. During the interval t_{high}, the output is high and C charges from an initial value of $V_{cc}(1 - 1/3A)/2$. The duty cycle for the circuit is given by $t_{high}/\tau = (R + R_d k)/(2R + R_d)$, where $\tau = t_{low} + t_{high}$ is the period of oscillation and k is a parameter controlled by the potentiometer R_d. The frequency of oscillation is

Random. A repeatable pseudorandom pulse train may be simulated by a dozen 74LS670 TTL RAMs. WD_0 through WD_{11} are the write-data lines and WA_0 through WA_3 are the address bits. The 1-MHz clock sets the width of the least significant bit to 1 μs. The flip-flops shape the output pulse, and the inverters detect the end of the pulse train.

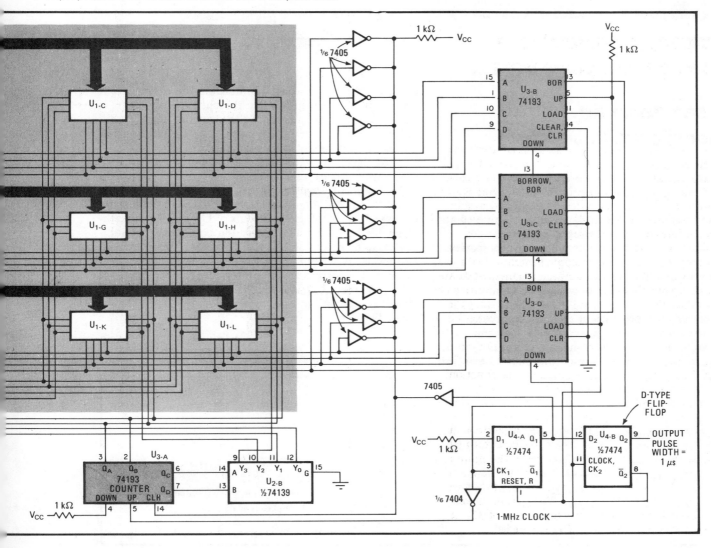

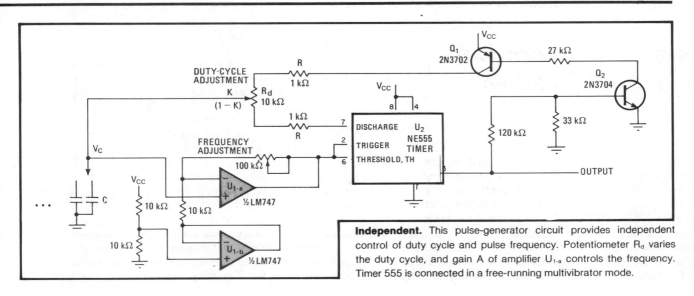

Independent. This pulse-generator circuit provides independent control of duty cycle and pulse frequency. Potentiometer R_d varies the duty cycle, and gain A of amplifier $U_{1\text{-}a}$ controls the frequency. Timer 555 is connected in a free-running multivibrator mode.

expressed as $f = 1/\tau = 3A/2C(R+R_d)$. The above relations for duty cycle and frequency show that the two can be controlled independently. Parameter k varies the duty cycle and gain A controls the frequency. The error in the approximation is about 4% at $A = 1$ and decreases rapidly with gain. In addition, the duty cycle varies linearly with the parameter k. ☐

TTL can generate composite video signals

by Kenneth P. Evans
College of Medicine, University of Cincinnati, Cincinnati, Ohio

Obtaining a composite video signal from discrete components is a difficult task. However, exclusive-NOR gates having open collector outputs and TTL compatibility end the problem since they eliminate the need to bias high-speed transistors or to interface digital and analog devices in systems where only character or graphics information is used.

The circuit (a) produces a quality composite video signal. The current through resistor R_1 determines the output voltage. When the sync pulse appears at the input, gate U_{1-a} pulls the output to ground. During the display portion of the horizontal scan, the black output level of 0.25 volt results when the output of gate U_{1-b} is held low. This voltage shunts the current through R_3. When the output of U_{1-b} is high, the current from R_3 passes through diode D_1 to increase the voltage across R_1 to 1 v—the color white on the cathode-ray tube.

Additional features may be incorporated in the design as shown in (b). Reverse video is obtained by supplying a logic 0 to the input of U_{2-b} when characters are displayed. Also, tying the outputs of U_{2-b} and U_{2-c} together enables the circuit to blank the characters. In addition, U_{2-d} helps switch the character brightness between two levels. When the output of U_{2-d} is high, the current through R_4 increases the amplitude of the video-dot voltage across R_1. The low output impedance of this circuit is compatible with the 75-ohm input of standard video displays. ☐

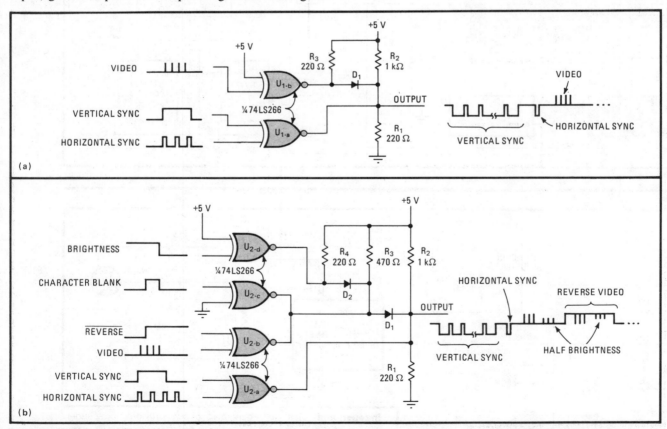

Composite video. Using exclusive-NOR gates with open collector outputs and TTL compatibility, the circuit (a) produces a quality composite video signal. The black output level is 0.25 volt and the white output level is 1 V. Adding more gates (b) provides such extra features as reverse video, character blanking, and two-level character brightness. In addition, the circuit's output impedance is low.

Delay circuit produces precision time intervals

by Jozef Kalisz
Warsaw, Poland

Using only four emitter-coupled-logic integrated circuits, this simple low-cost time-delay generator produces precise time intervals between start and stop pulses and creates a pulse whose width is controlled by the preset delay. The output delay can be adjusted in clock-period increments.

Initially, two out of six D-type flip-flops contained in U_2 are set by the synchronization pulse. Also, the clock pulse sets the $\overline{Q}$ output at pin 15 of U_2 to a low level, which is inverted by gates G_1 and G_2. This inverted output presets flip-flops U_{1-a} and U_{1-b} and in addition provides the starting pulse. The rising edge of the next clock pulse terminates the starting pulse and shifts the low state to pin 11 of U_2. Subsequently, the successive

clock pulses shift the low state in sequence from one to another. These $\overline{Q}$ outputs are inverted by gates G_3 and G_4 to provide the stop pulse. Since pins 13 and 15 are set simultaneously, the output at pin 13 produces zero delay.

The leading edges of the start and stop pulses are directly related to the falling edges of the appropriate clock pulses. The duration of the output pulses is determined by the low state of the clock pulse, and the time interval between the start and stop pulses is selected by means of switch S_1. The range attained with this circuit is 0 to 10τ in increments of τ, where τ is the period of the clock input.

The pulse generated at the width output has a duration equal to the preset delay. The three outputs, whose repetition frequency is determined by the frequency of the sync input signal, can directly drive 50-ohm loads. The time-delay accuracy is better than 100 picoseconds and depends mainly on the propagation delay introduced by the gates. Also, the circuit requires that the external clock and sync source must have ECL outputs. □

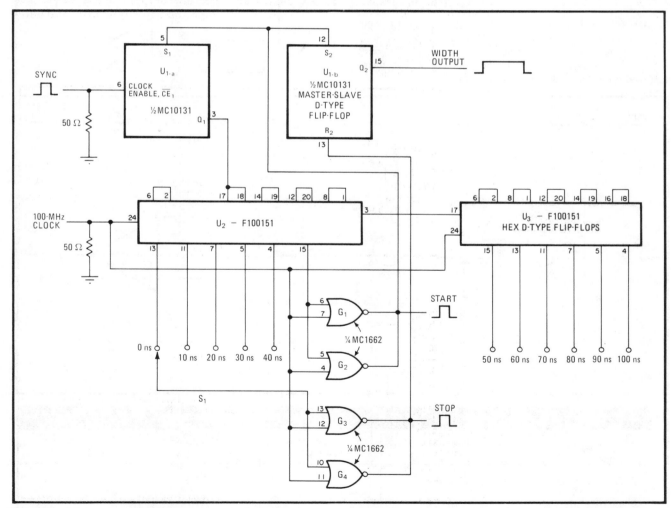

Selectable. This pulse-delay generator provides selectable time intervals, in steps of 10 nanoseconds, between the start and stop pulses. For a clock input of 100 megahertz, the range covered by the circuit is 0 to 100 ns with an accuracy of better than 100 picoseconds. The pulse generated at the width output has a duration equal to the preset delay. The external clock and sync source must have ECL outputs.

Canceling cusps on the peaks of shaped sine waves

by Stephen H. Burns
United States Naval Academy, Annapolis, Md.

Most triangle-to-sine-wave converters employed in a function generator are incapable of reducing cusps on the output peaks, so that discontinuities occur in the derivative. This design (Fig. 1a) subtracts a portion of the triangular wave from a shaped sine wave. As a result, the slope at the wave's peak can be reduced to zero with negligible harmonic distortion. In addition, the design is insensitive to the occurrence of small changes in triangular-wave amplitude.

Results for three different wave shapers are shown in

Shaper. This negative feedforward scheme (a) subtracts traingular components from sine waves and cancels cusps of their peaks. The scheme is implemented with a differential amplifier (b). Op amp U_1 subtracts the triangular wave from the sine-wave output, thereby suppressing odd harmonics by more than 52 dB.

the table. Because the differential amplifier has the lowest distortion and highest bandwidth, it is presented as an example (Fig. 1b).

Operational amplifier U_1 subtracts the triangular-wave input from the shaped sine wave, and resistors R_1 and R_2 control the amount of negative feedforward. The differential amplifier, functioning as the shaper, consists of transistors Q_1 and Q_2. Any differences in transistor characteristics, which develop even-order harmonic distortion at the output, is adjusted with resistors R_4, R_5, and R_6. Finally, R_7 and R_8 feed the shaped signal to the noninverting input of U_1.

The circuit's performance has been measured with a spectrum analyzer. It suppresses odd harmonics by more than 52 decibels. □

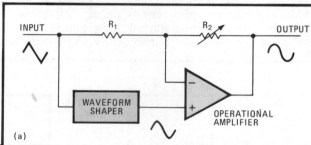

(a)

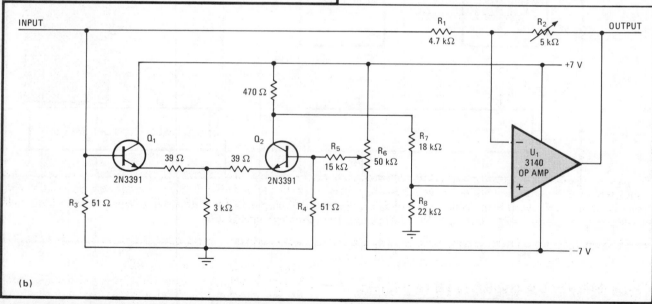

(b)

OPERATING CHARACTERISTICS OF THREE WAVEFORM SHAPERS				
Shaper	Triangular-wave input (V p-p)	Sine-wave output (V p-p)	Total harmonic distortion (%)	Frequency (kHz) at 2% THD
Four-diode type	3.45	2.400	0.7	150
Field-effect transistor	2.48	0.072	0.6	40
Differential amplifier	0.38	0.560	0.4	200

Three-chip circuit produces longer one-shot delays

by Samuel C. Creason
Beckman Instruments Inc., Fullerton, Calif.

One-shot delays of more than a few minutes are difficult to obtain without high RC timing values. However, this three-chip circuit multiplies a one-shot's delay to produce lapses of up to 160 minutes with just a 715-kilohm resistor and a 1-microfarad capacitor. In addition, the circuit can produce even longer delays without changing the values of R and C.

Once the circuit is turned on, counter U_1 is reset and remains in that state until a low level is applied to the input terminal. When the input is low, U_1 begins to count the negative edges of a 1-hertz pulse train that is generated by astable multivibrator U_2. To obtain a specific delay, the appropriate counter output is connected to the input of U_{3-a} as shown in the figure.

When U_1 has counted the clock pulses required to produce the desired delay, the jumper-selected output of U_1 goes high and U_2 is reset. In turn, the output terminal, which had been high, then goes low. The circuit remains in this state until the low level is removed from the input.

Longer delays of any duration may be obtained by inserting an appropriate divider between the output of U_2 and clock input of U_1. □

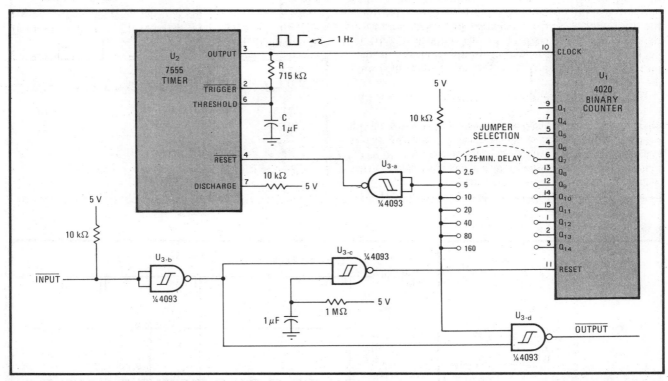

Prolonged. Using three chips, this circuit produces one-shot delays of up to 160 minutes with just a resistor and a capacitor as timing elements. Astable multivibrator U_2 generates clock pulses for counter U_1. The output of U_1 is tied to the appropriate delay input of U_{3-a}, and U_2 is reset when U_1's jumper-selected output goes high. This state change makes the output go low.

Thumbwheel switch programs retriggerable one-shot

by Dil Sukh Jain
National Remote Sensing Agency, Hyderabad, India

This programmable synchronous one-shot is a few jumps ahead of the rest by being able to generate a synchronized output pulse whose width can be varied through an externally controlled clock period or a programmable thumbwheel switch. In addition, the circuit is retriggerable with a provision for a clear input.

A narrow negative pulse applied at the trigger input loads the synchronous binary-coded–decimal down-up counter 74190 with the number (N) set on the thumbwheel switch and simultaneously sets Q_1 of flip-flop A_1 high. This loading in turn sets Q_2 of flip-flop A_2 high. The low level at $\overline{Q_1}$ enables the counter to count down from N on successive positive edges of the clock.

When the counter reaches zero, a negative pulse is produced at the ripple clock output of the counter 74190, which corresponds to the negative edge of the clock. This negative pulse, inverted by the 7404 chip, triggers A_1 to make Q_1 low and the enable ($\overline{Q_1}$) input high, which in turn disables the counter and inhibits the circuit. The

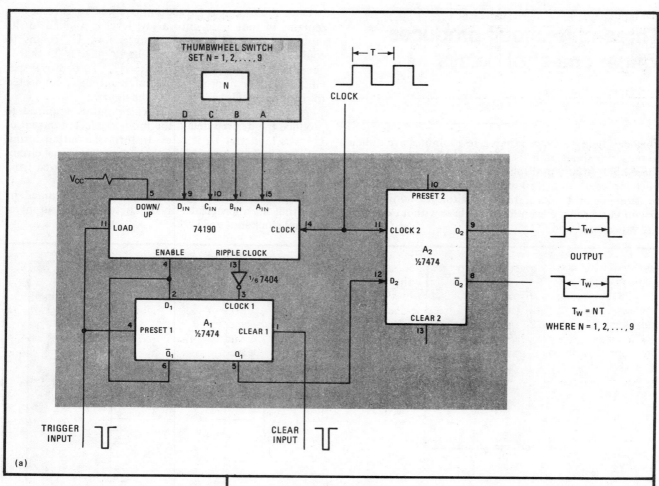

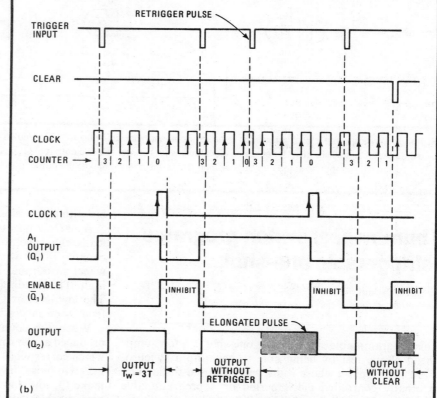

Programmable one-shot. The output pulse width of this synchronized one-shot (a) is programmed with a thumbwheel switch. The circuit uses a binary-coded–decimal counter 74190 and D type flip-flop 7474 to provide the retrigger and clear feature. The timing diagram (b) for N = 3 illustrates the control of retrigger and clear inputs on the output pulse.

low input level at D_2 terminates the output pulse whose width is given by $T_w = NT$, where T is the clock's period. The one-shot output pulse width when N = 3 is 3T(b).

A retrigger pulse applied while the counter is counting down reloads the circuit with set number N and begins a new countdown, resulting in a single stretched pulse at output Q_2. A negative pulse applied at the clear input (while the counter is counting down) terminates the output pulse at the clock's following positive edge.   □

Synchronous one-shot has integral pulse width

by Robert D. Guyton
Mississippi State University, Starkville, Miss.

The pulse width of a one-shot multivibrator is usually adjusted with variable RC elements. However, this synchronous one-shot uses three integrated circuits to generate a pulse whose width is an integral multiple of the input clock period. The accuracy of the one-shot's pulse width depends on that of the input clock frequency.

The circuit uses switch S_1 to select pulse widths ranging from 1 to 10 clock periods wide. Starting at logic state 1111, synchronous 4-bit counter U_2 resumes counting when input pulse P(b) triggers the one-shot circuit. The input pulse can be synchronized with the clock or may be asynchronous. The width of the asynchronous pulse must be about 1.5 times the clock's period. Because the logic is connected to the enable-p input of U_2, the counting continues until the input-to-load function of U_2 is set low. This low resets the counter to the 1111 state where it waits for another input.

The load input for U_2 is obtained from the selected output of the binary-coded-decimal–to–decimal decoder U_3, which in turn gives the selection of pulse widths ranging from 1 to 10 clock periods wide. The combination of waveforms Z and P, using gates U_{1-a} through U_{1-d}, enable the counter.

If only one output pulse width is required, the circuit may be modified by replacing U_3 and S_1 with a single NAND gate having the appropriate inputs.   □

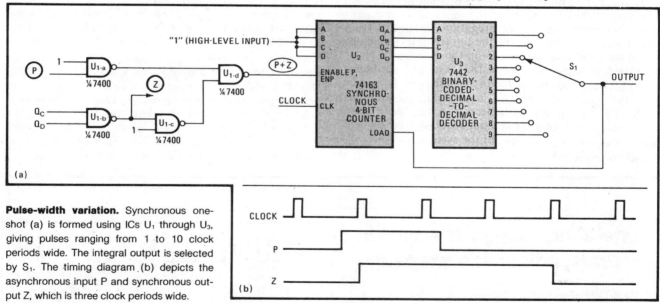

Pulse-width variation. Synchronous one-shot (a) is formed using ICs U_1 through U_3, giving pulses ranging from 1 to 10 clock periods wide. The integral output is selected by S_1. The timing diagram (b) depicts the asynchronous input P and synchronous output Z, which is three clock periods wide.

Comparator, one-shot produce pulse-width inversion for servos

by John Karasz
Norden Systems, Norwalk, Conn.

Frequencies usually trigger movements of servo-actuators within radio-controlled vehicles. However, these transmitted waves are difficult to produce and are noisy.

This design overcomes both problems by employing pulse control with a comparator, two monostable multivibrators, and a pair of NOR gates. Although the circuit produces only three pulses, or three servo positions, more comparators and NOR gates may be added to create an n-position control.

The circuit compares the width of the input pulse with that of a reference. A reference pulse of 1.5 milliseconds is selected for the circuit through the RC network connected to one-shot U_{1a}. As a result, pulse durations of 1.0 ms and 2.0 ms produce servo-output positions of $+45°$ and $-45°$, respectively.

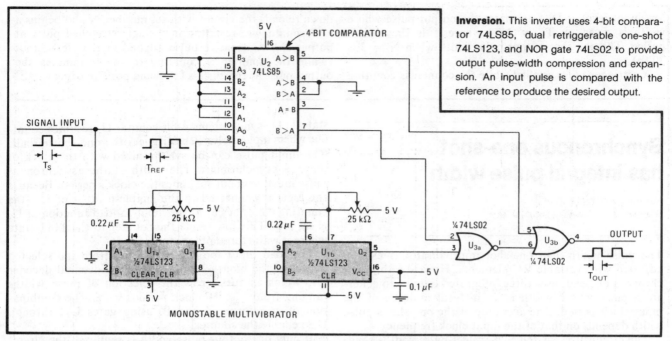

Inversion. This inverter uses 4-bit comparator 74LS85, dual retriggerable one-shot 74LS123, and NOR gate 74LS02 to provide output pulse-width compression and expansion. An input pulse is compared with the reference to produce the desired output.

The reference pulse is triggered by the leading edge of the input pulse. The trailing edge of this pulse triggers U_{1b} to generate output Q_2, which is equal in duration to its input. When the width of the input pulse is equal to the reference pulse, output Q_2 passes through the NOR gates and is unchanged. Under this condition, no contributions are made by the comparator outputs.

However, when the width of the input pulse is greater than the reference pulse, the trailing edge of Q_1 triggers U_{1b} and comparator U_2 produces a high output at pin $5(A > B)$. This pulse starts at the trailing edge of the reference pulse and ends at the falling edge of the input pulse, thereby resulting in an output pulse of duration equal to the width of the reference minus the width of comparator output $A > B$.

Lastly, when the input-pulse width is shorter than the reference, the comparator generates a $B > A$ output at pin 7. Its duration begins at the trailing edge of the input pulse and terminates at the falling edge of the reference pulse. The Q_2 pulse of U_{1b} and $B > A$ output of the comparator are fed to gate U_{3a}, which generates an output of equal in duration to the width of the reference plus the width of comparator output $B > A$. Mirror-image pulse widths are produced about the reference pulse and the output is thus defined by $T_{out} = T_q \pm |T_s - T_{ref}|$, where T_{out} is the width of the output pulse, T_q is the duration of one-shot U_{1b}, T_s is the duration of the input, and T_{ref} is the width of the reference pulse. □

Generating triangular waves in accurate, adjustable shapes

by Virgil Tiponut and Adrian Stoian
Timisoara, Romania

Many precision instruments and generators require adjustable and well-defined triangular waveforms that have very accurate peak values. However, most of today's triangular-waveform generators lack features permitting simple parameter modification. This circuit allows these generators to overcome this shortcoming and provides the means for high resolution and speed

1. Precision. The circuit (a) built with comparators U_1 and U_2, constant current sources, and switch S_1 generates a triangular waveform (b) whose peak value, rise, and fall can be selected. The comparators determine the charge and discharge of capacitor C.

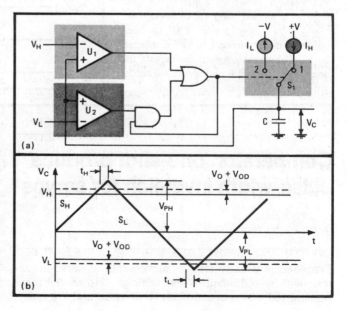

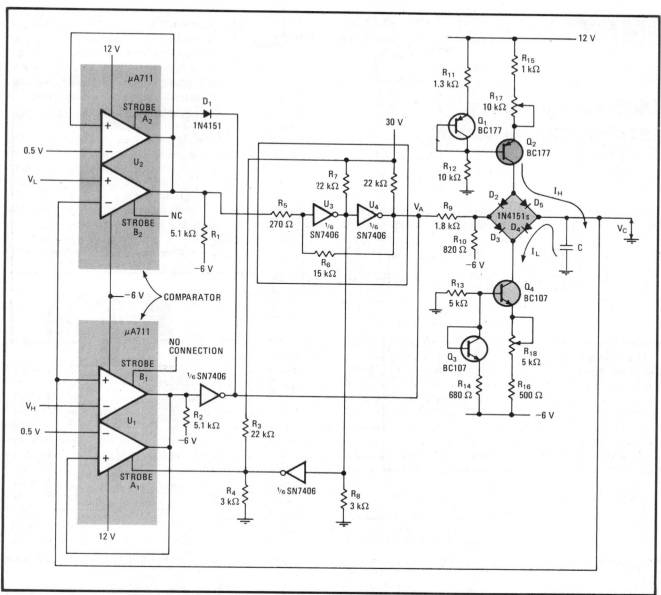

2. Adjustable generator. High speed and resolution, in addition to peak values that can be controlled, are obtained for this triangular-waveform generator by dual voltage comparators U_1 and U_2, which have positive feedback. Charging and discharging of capacitor C is controlled through strobe A_1 and strobe A_2. Inverters U_3 and U_4 are used to improve the switching time.

along with controllable peak, rise, and fall values.

Comparators U_1 and U_2 (Fig. 1a) having threshold voltages V_h and V_l, respectively, determine the charge and discharge rates of capacitor C. When switch S_1 is in position 1, the constant current I_h charges C. In position 2, the capacitor discharges current I_l. The resulting triangular waveform (Fig. 1b) shows that the peak, rise, and fall of V_c can be easily varied through the adjustment of threshold levels V_h and V_l and I_h and I_l.

The resultant error for V_h and V_l, respectively, is $e_h \leq V_o + V_{od} + t_h S_h$ and $e_l \leq V_o + V_{od} + t_l S_l$, where V_o is the input offset voltage of the comparators, t_h and t_l are the settling times for the high and low states corresponding to an overdrive voltage V_{od}, and S_h and S_l represent the slopes of V_c.

A dual voltage comparator $\mu A711$ having positive feedback provides high resolution and good propagation times (Fig. 2). When input voltage V_c goes above V_h, comparator U_1 is switched to a high state and remains in it, irrespective of the value of V_c, until a low level is applied to strobe input A_1. In this high state, current source Q_2 charges C with current I_h.

As a result, U_1 lowers the value of V_a, which, in turn, causes the capacitor to discharge I_l through transistor Q_4. While the capacitor is in the course of discharging, comparator U_2 switches to the low state because the voltage at strobe A_2 is low.

The discharge process continues until V_c drops below V_l. Once this drop occurs, comparator U_2 goes high. As a result, the output voltage of U_2 and consequently V_a will go high again. Thus the cycle repeats. Inverters U_3 and U_4 are connected as a Schmitt trigger to improve switching time, and D_2 through D_4 serve as a switch. Diode D_1 limits the strobe voltage when V_a is high. ☐

INSTRUMENT CIRCUITS

Digital weighing scale resolves quarter counts

by David Watson
Intersil Datel (UK) Ltd., Basingstoke, Hants., England

By using a display-driving counter and adding three flip-flops, it is possible to quadruple the resolution of a low-cost digital weighing scale (Fig. 1a). The rest of the scale's circuitry is standard, consisting of a strain-gage transducer, a complementary-MOS amplifier, and an analog-to-digital converter. Since the revised circuit is designed to resolve to a quarter of a displayed increment, the scale displays N/4 for an N-count conversion.

The a-d converter has three phases of operation. In the automatic zeroing phase, offset is measured and nullified and the busy output is low. During the integrating phase, the busy output goes high and the converter integrates the input signal for 10,000 clock cycles. Finally, the deintegrating cycle integrates the reference until the integrator returns to its starting, or zero-crossing, point. For a digital reading of N, the deintegration lasts for N + 1 clock cycles, at the end of which the busy signal

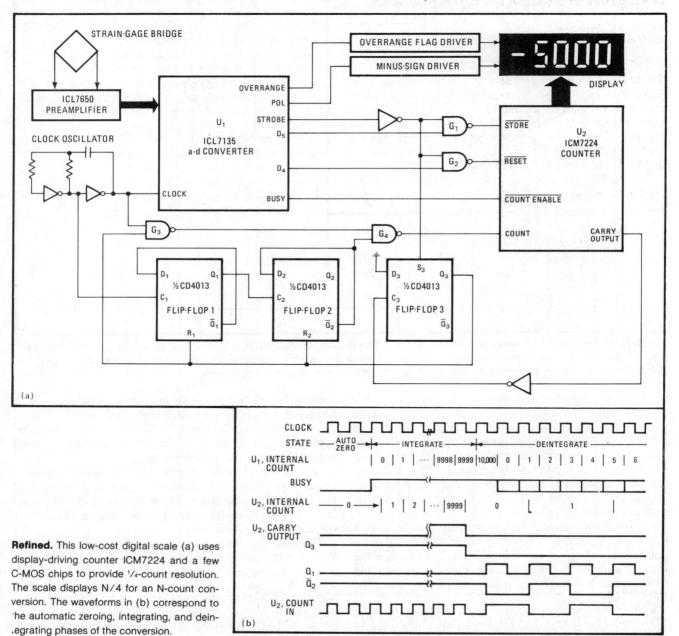

(a)

(b)

Refined. This low-cost digital scale (a) uses display-driving counter ICM7224 and a few C-MOS chips to provide ¼-count resolution. The scale displays N/4 for an N-count conversion. The waveforms in (b) correspond to the automatic zeroing, integrating, and deintegrating phases of the conversion.

returns low. The busy output is therefore high for a total of 10,001 + N clock cycles.

The N/4 display is obtained by delaying for 10,001 clock cycles after the busy output of converter U_1 goes high and then enabling the counter U_2 to increment at ¼ the converter clock rate. The counter is halted as soon as the busy signal goes low and its contents are transferred to the display. The reset pulse now sets the converter ready for the next cycle.

During auto zero, the busy output is low (b) and the counter is disabled. The Q_3 output of flip-flop 3 enables gate G_3, which allows the U_1 clock pulses to go to counter U_2. The counter begins to increment at the start of the integrating phase. After 10,000 counts, the falling edge of carry output of U_2 clocks flip-flop 3 to its reset state. The other two flip-flops are now enabled and divide the input clock by 4 while G_3 blocks the direct clock input to the counter, which has now returned to zero. The strobe output of U_1 generates the pulse necessary to store the count in U_2 and then reset U_2. □

Doubling the resolution of a digital waveform synthesizer

by David M. Weigand
West Chester, Pa.

There seem to be almost as many ways of generating waveforms as there are applications. However, symmetrical waveforms such as sine or triangular waves generated by digital synthesizers can be improved by incorporating a simple operational-amplifier circuit. With this circuit, the resolution of the output waveform is doubled and its distortion substantially reduced.

The standard waveform generator (a) consists of a digital-to-analog converter driven by a read-only memory and a counter that provides sequential addresses for the ROM. It is modified (b) by replacing the M-bit counter with an (M + 1)-bit counter and placing the op amp circuit between the converter and the low-pass filter, whose gain is also doubled. This modification halves the staircase step of the output waveform and thereby also doubles its resolution.

Only half of the sine wave is stored in ROM U_2. Input frequency f_{in} is doubled so that converter U_3 outputs two triangular waves of amplitude V_{dr} each quantized in N bits. Alternate halves of V_{dr} are flipped using transistor Q_1 and an (M + 1) count of counter U_1.

The output of operational amplifier U_4 is alternately ground and $-(3/2)V_{dr}$. This output is continuously summed with V_{dr} using two 10-kilohm resistors, which results in $V_x = \pm V_{dr}/2$. The V_x signal is fed into the filter U_5 to obtain the desired output waveform V_{od} with greatly reduced distortion. □

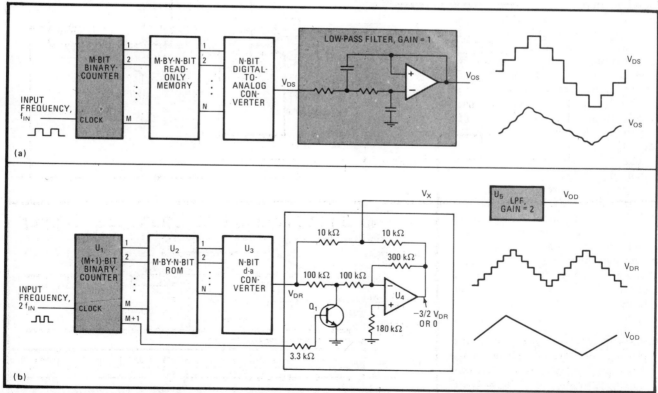

Higher resolution. The resolution of the standard ROM–plus–data-converter symmetric-waveform generator (a) can be doubled by incorporating in it a few simple changes—using an (M + 1)-bit instead of an M-bit counter and employing an op-amp circuit between the converted and the filter (b). In addition, the input frequency is twice f_{in}. The output waveforms for the two circuits are as shown.

Two-chip ammeter measures currents down to picoamperes

by Douglas Modlin
Electrical Engineering Department, Stanford University, Stanford, Calif.

An ammeter circuit that can measure currents ranging from picoamperes to amperes may be built with two operational amplifiers, one having a low input bias current and offset voltage and the second having a high output-current capability. The accuracy of the meter is within 1%.

The basic configuration of the circuit (a) establishes A_1 as a field-effect–transistor input device that is internally compensated and A_2 as the power stage. The feedback arrangement of the circuit is technically possible but not practical because A_2's gain-bandwidth product is much less than that of A_1. This factor is due to A_2's high-output capacity. As a consequence, the circuit is unstable and oscillates near the unity-gain crossover point of A_2, because of a phase-shift around the feedback loop exceeding 360°.

Converting A_1 into an integrating comparator (b) stabilizes the circuit, thereby increasing the op amp's response time without introducing an additional phase shift to the feedback loop. Input current I_{in} flowing to the noninverting terminal of A_1 produces a positive voltage at its output and across integrating capacitor C_1. A_2, serving as an inverting, unity-gain amplifier, then raises its output to a voltage that causes I_f to equal I_{in}.

As a result, the output voltage corresponding to this input current is $V_o = -I_{in}R_f$. The circuit accuracy is determined strictly by the tolerance of R_f. The input offset voltage of A_1 (1 millivolt maximum) and its correspondingly low offset current (0.15 picoampere maximum) have virtually no adverse effect on circuit accuracy. As for A_2's output offset voltage, which is a maximum of 6 mV, it is canceled in the feedback loop. In order to maintain a virtual short at its input, A_1 develops a voltage across C_1. When this voltage is applied to A_2 through R_2, A_2's offset voltage is canceled. This cancellation effect is independent of the second stage gain given by $A = -R_3/R_2$.

Feedback resistor R_f sets the cur-

rent range. To measure currents in the region of 1 pA for display on a 3½-digit digital voltmeter (resolution is 1 mV), R_f should be 10^9 ohms and be proportionally lower for higher currents. The circuit's input port A_1, should be protected against leakage currents by Teflon standoffs or otherwise be guarded. This measure also holds true for mounting the selectable resistor R_f.

The circuit in (c) is much the same as in (b), but is configured as a low-input bias current, low-offset buffer amplifier whose gain is established by $A = R_3/R_2$. This circuit takes advantage of the best features of both op amps but suppresses their limitations. Including resistor R_o in the circuit will stabilize the amplifier for capacitive loads. Incidentally, the LH0041 allows a user to select current limiting. The circuits discussed are not limited to the op amps listed in the figures. Any device with similar characteristics may be used. □

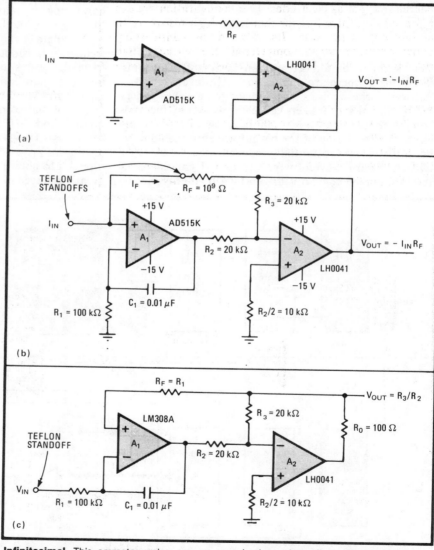

Infinitesimal. This ammeter, using one op amp having a low offset and another with a high-output driver, measures current from 1 pA to 1 A. Feedback resistor R_f determines the range of measurement. Based on the rudimentary circuit of (a), ammeter (b) is self-compensating and stable, providing accuracy to within 1%. Test currents are converted to corresponding voltage for display by 3½-digit digital voltmeter. A version for measuring low potentials (c) is similar. The LH0041 op amp allows users to select current limiting.

Conductive foam forms reliable pressure sensor

by Thomas Henry
Transonic Laboratories, Mankato, Minn.

Pressure-sensitive resistors made with conductive foam usually suffer from mechanical and electrical reliability problems—the electrodes of the unit are prone to short, and its sensor rarely returns to its initial value once the pressure is released. However, this circuit, which uses a low-cost electronic pressure sensor, overcomes these problems and provides additional control voltages.

The electronic pressure sensor (a) comprises a conductive foam that is sandwiched between two copper-clad boards that act as electrodes. This configuration creates a pressure-sensitive resistor that has a high resistance in an uncompressed state. Its value drops considerably under pressure; when compressed, the sensor's high resistance value of 10 to 50 kilohms drops to several hundred ohms.

Sensor. This pressure-sensitive resistor (a) together with the circuit (b) provides a reliable electronic pressure sensor. Conductive foam that is sandwiched between two electrodes forms the pressure sensor. Ordinary insulating foam rubber, surrounding the conductive layer, is placed within the sandwich to prevent the boards from shorting. The output from the sensor is sensed by op amp A_1.

The insulating foam rubber placed in the sandwich prevents the electrodes from shorting and also evens out the action of the sensor. Common integrated-circuit packaging foam is used as the conductive material.

Operational amplifier A_1 senses the output generated by voltage divider R_6 and the pressure sensor (b). Any noise in the system is grounded by capacitor C_1. In addition, C_3 functions as a low-pass filter to provide a smooth voltage at the output of A_1. When the pressure sensor has a nominal uncompressed resistance of 10 kΩ, the voltage at pin 3 of A_1 is about -5 volts when the sensor is uncompressed and -15 v when compressed. This voltage swing is offset by a fixed value of $+7.5$ v,

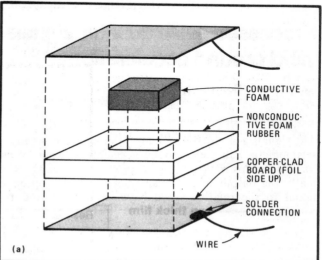

(a)

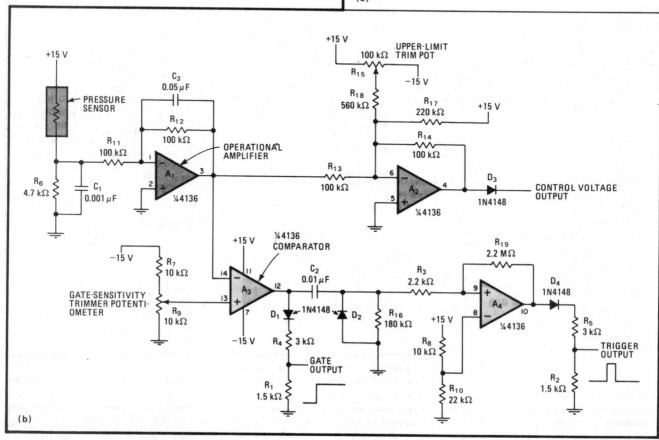

(b)

produced by R_{17}, and the sum is inverted by A_2 whose output then swings from -2.5 v to $+7.5$ v. In addition, this output is further truncated by diode D_3 to provide a range of 0 to $+7$ v. As a result, the sensor will always indicate a return to a constant value.

Comparator A_3 generates a gate output that is based on the amount of pressure exerted on the pad, which is set by trimmer potentiometer R_9. The comparator output is differentiated by A_4 to provide a 1-millisecond, 5-v trigger pulse.

This circuit is designed to control an electronic-music synthesizer. The control-voltage output of the circuit controls the voltage-controlled oscillator while the gate and trigger pulses fire the envelope generator of the synthesizer. Thus one transducer is used to control several parameters of a design simultaneously.

Though the circuit provides a reliable uncompressed and compressed voltage output, there is no guarantee that the voltages between these two extremes follow a linear progression. The plot of the voltages depends both on the physics of the sensor and the voltage drop across diode D_3.   □

Processed seismometer signals yield ground acceleration

by Thomas D. Roberts
Department of Electrical Engineering, University of Alaska, Fairbanks

The signals generated by a conventional electromagnetic seismometer can yield ground acceleration when transformed by this real-time signal processor (Fig. 1). Normally the output of the seismometer, which is proportional to the relative speed between its case and the suspended seismic mass, bears little resemblance to the input excitation. Thus the ideal but unlikely case of sinusoidal ground acceleration is the only condition in which the seismometer output is proportional to ground acceleration.

However, the output (Fig. 2a) of a typical short-period seismometer due to a step excitation has a natural frequency of 1 hertz with a damping factor of 0.4, and this can be obtained by removing a known weight from the suspended seismic mass of the seismometer. This signal is analyzed by the signal processor to enable the system to track the ground acceleration accurately.

Using the concept presented by Berckhemer and Schneider,[1] the processor's differential equation is:

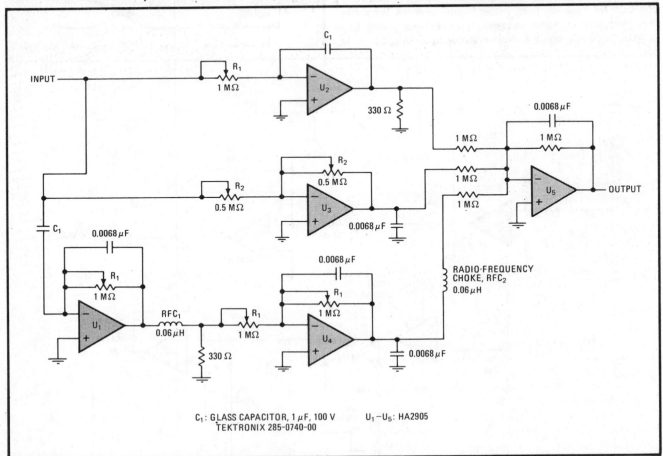

1. Seismic. This real-time signal processor tracks ground acceleration accurately. For accuracy and high performance, the circuit uses chopper-stabilized, high-input impedance operational amplifiers with excellent offset drift characteristics.

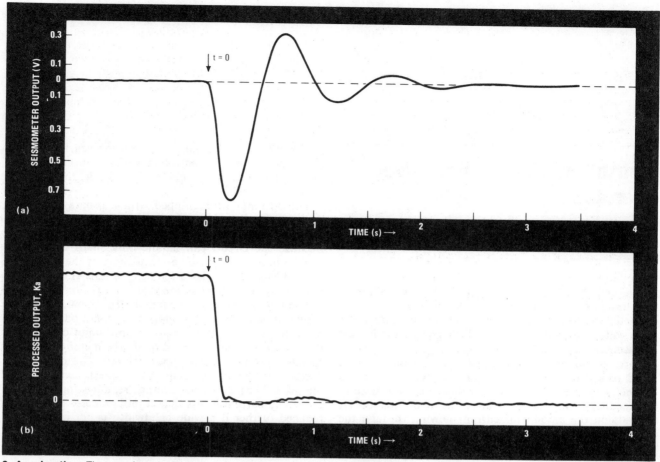

2. Acceleration. The waveform in (a) is the response of a short-period seismometer to a step-function input. The step response of the processed seismometer signal (b) resembles the step input excitation. The rise time is about 120 milliseconds, with 3% maximum overshoot.

$$Kd^3y/dt^3 = d^2e/dt^2 + 2\zeta\omega_n \, de/dt + \omega_n^2 e$$

where

K = the gain constant
y = the vertical displacement of the seismic mass
ω_n = the natural frequency
e = the voltage output of the seismometer
ζ = its damping factor.

The processor provides the exact reciprocal of the seismometer transfer function. The true ground acceleration parallel to the seismometer axis is obtained by integration of the above equation, which yields:

$$\frac{d^2y}{dt^2} = \frac{1}{K}\left\{\frac{de}{dt} + 2\zeta\omega_n e + \omega_n^2 \int_0^t e\,dt\right\}$$

This relationship is determined by the processor with satisfactory accuracy only if it uses modern, monolithic chopper-stabilized operational amplifiers with high input impedance and excellent offset characteristics. Op amps U_1–U_5 employ Harris Semiconductor's HA-2905.

The circuit malfunctions without the use of the recommended op amps. The right values for resistances R_1 and R_2 are obtained by trial and error for a given model of seismometer. The processed seismometer output is a step signal of high quality with a maximum overshoot of about 3% (Fig. 2b). This output response is due to a step input excitation of the seismometer. □

References
1. H. Berckhemer and G. Schneider, "Near Earthquakes Recorded with Long Period Seismometers," Bulletin of the Seismological Society of America, 1964, pp. 54 and 973.

Instrumentation-meter driver operates on 2-V supply

by David M. Barnett and Everett L. Tindall
Martin Marietta Aerospace, Denver, Colo.

Complementary-MOS operational amplifiers and a bridge circuit, employed as a feedback loop, minimize the number of parts needed to build an accurate ac and dc meter that operates from a 2-volt supply. The meter has a wide bandwidth, consumes little power, and is used in testing cables in missile interfaces.

Three amplifiers, U_1 through U_3, are connected in a standard instrumentation configuration, while U_4 acts as the meter's driver. A full-wave rectifier bridge is used in the feedback loop of U_4. Since the operation of U_4 depends on the amount of current flowing through the bridge, diode voltage drops do not alter the circuit's

performance. Under normal operation, current I_{in} = I_{meter}, and both are controlled with potentiometer R_8. Optional capacitor C_2 makes it possible to limit the meter's bandwidth.

The op amps are equipped with a programming pin that sets standby current I_q. Pulling these pins low sets I_q for maximum frequency response and current output. Because the circuit can handle only small currents, it may be necessary to use pnp transistors at the outputs of U_3 and U_4 if the full-scale meter current is high. Also, low-leakage diodes must be selected for the bridge.

The circuit requires a minimal adjustment. While R_6 allows adjustment of the input common-mode rejection ratio, R_{13} compensates for all op-amp input offsets, and R_8 provides a full-scale reading on the meter that corresponds to the full-scale input voltage. The circuit's 3-decibel bandwidth exceeds 50 kilohertz when C_2 is removed. The meter gives average readings for ac inputs. Its supply current is less than 8 milliamperes and can be reduced further if a wide bandwidth is not required by adjusting I_q. □

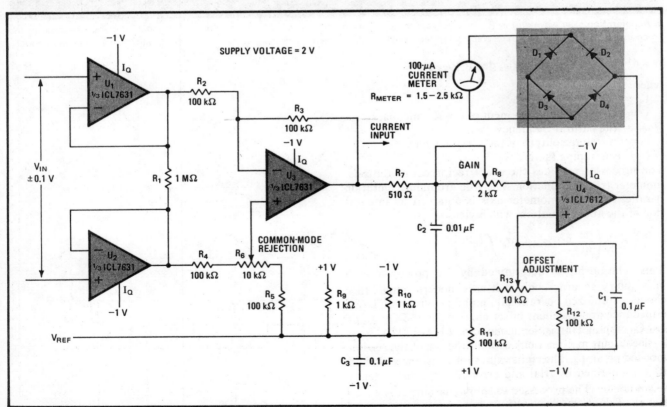

Low power. This instrumentation-meter driver uses complementary-MOS operational amplifiers U_1 through U_4 and a bridge rectifier to provide a design that can operate on a 2-volt supply. The meter scale is adjusted using resistor R_8, while capacitor C_2 permits bandwidth limiting. Under normal operation, current I_{in} equals I_{meter}.

Measuring irregular waveforms by detecting amplitude changes

by Jeffrey Schenkel
Norwood, Mass.

When respiratory rates or other types of irregular waveforms are measured, it is often desirable to record just the change in the signal amplitude and leave out baseline variations and noise. This circuit does the job with only a baker's dozen of parts.

First, input waveform voltage V_{input} directs voltage V_x. In addition, the output voltages of operational amplifiers A_1 and A_2 are negative and positive power-supply rails. This arrangement forces diodes D_1 and D_2 into a reverse-biased condition and in turn couples the input signal to the op amps' inverting inputs.

As the input voltage increases, V_x eclipses the threshold voltage, V_{th}, which is set by an external source. Once this swing occurs, the output of A_2 begins to go negative until D_2 turns on, which prevents V_x from becoming more positive. V_{in} now begins to decline from its peak, D_2 shuts off, and V_x follows V_{in} in a negative direction until $V_x = 0$ volt. As a result, the output of A_1 begins to swing positive and turns on D_1, preventing V_x from going negative. Finally, when V_{in} reaches its negative peak, D_1 turns off and the cycle begins again.

Output voltages V_{A_1} and V_{A_2} of op amps A_1 and A_2 indicate negative and positive signal excursions (b). These signals are then combined and fed to the Schmitt trigger. The output of A_3 changes state only when V_x hits 0 V or the threshold voltage, and it completes a cycle when the input signal experiences both a negative and positive voltage swing that is equal to at least the threshold voltage.

V_{output} can be fed to edge-triggered circuitry for rate counting or other processing. As the system uses the highest peaks and lowest troughs to determine the excursion size, it is not fooled by small signal reversals. □

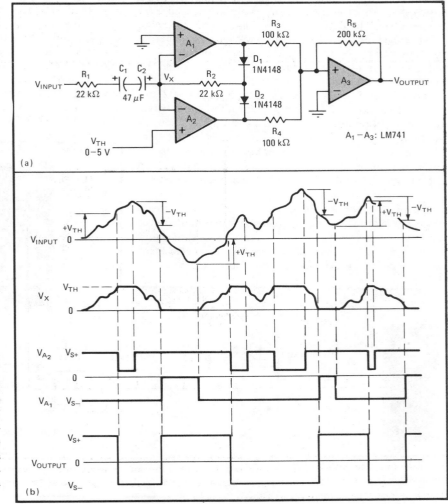

Detector. The output voltages of operational amplifiers A_1 and A_2 in the circuit in (a) are combined and fed to the Schmitt trigger A_3. The output of A_3, V_{output}, indicates the negative and positive changes in amplitude of the input waveform. Also, the threshold level is set by an external voltage. Various waveforms generated by the circuit that correspond to the input are shown in (b).

Building a low-cost optical time-domain reflectometer

by J. T. Harvey, G. D. Sizer, and N. S. Turnbull
AWA Research Laboratory, North Ryde, NSW, Australia

High-performance optical time-domain reflectometers require relatively complex optics and are fairly expensive—around $4,000 to $20,000. However, if a little accuracy can be sacrificed, this simple-to-use time-domain reflectometer, at a cost of only $500, can handily substitute for its more expensive brethren.

Designed primarily to locate faults in and measure losses of optical fibers, this device (a) uses a commercially available optical-fiber coupler, type TC4C. A light pulse is applied to the end of the fiber that is undergoing analysis, and imperfections in the cable are sensed by a photodetector. The detector [*Electronics,* Sept. 25, 1980, p. 161] measures the generated backscattered energy. Once detected with the TDR, this energy pulse is analyzed to determine the nature of the defect and its location on the fiber.

International Telephone & Telegraph's LA10-02 single heterostructure laser diode, which radiates at a wavelength of 905 nanometers, is used as the optical source. This diode is mounted into an Amp Inc. optimate connector and pulsed at a peak current of 25 amperes by six field-effect transistors that are connected in parallel. In addition, a fiber tail with a 100-micrometer-diameter

core latched to port 4 of the optical coupler is plugged into the other end of the connector.

The receiving fiber tail is similarly coupled to a Siemens SFH202 p-i-n photodetector plugged into a photodiode amplifier. This 2.2-megohm transimpedance amplifier with a bandwidth of 5 megahertz uses in its input stage a MOS FET BF960, which is followed by a voltage amplifier with a gain of 30. In addition, proper layout reduces stray coupling and interference.

Port 2 of the coupler is index-matched with oil or a glycerin-water mixture that will absorb the reflection occurring at the end of the fiber tail. Port 1 is connected to the fiber under test. Because the fiber used in the coupler is wide, an Amp optimate connector bushing and a pair of AMP227285-4 connectors may be used as the joint between the two fibers. The connection is index-matched to minimize the front-face reflection.

An oscilloscope is used to read the location of splices or imperfections in the fiber under test. The magnitude of optical loss over a specified distance is obtained by estimating the backscatter (b) at each of the two points selected and calculating the loss—5 log V_1/V_2 decibels, where V_1 and V_2 represent the backscatter at the two selected measuring points. For example, when a laser with a peak power of 7 dBm is coupled into a test fiber having a core diameter of 50 μm, the fiber's backscatter at 1 kilometer was found to be 3 to 5 nanowatts and was observed for over 5 km of low-loss fiber. □

Inexpensive. This optical time-domain reflectometer (a) uses a commercially available Canstar 100-μm-diameter core step-index optical coupler to substantially lower the cost of the instrument yet maintains a satisfactory performance level. The scope photograph (b) shows measurable backscatter for 5 km of fiber under test.

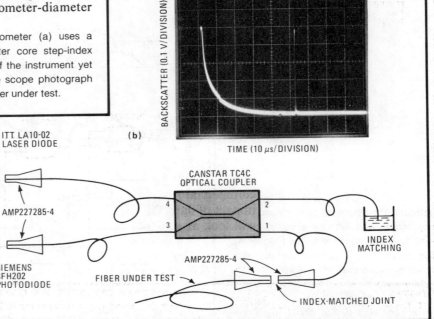

Ac voltmeter measures
FET dynamic transconductance

by M. J. Salvati
Flushing Communications, Flushing, N. Y.

Instruments used to test field-effect transistors and MOS FETs make either static transconductance measurements or no transconductance measurements at all. However, when this simple test circuit is combined with a standard ac voltmeter, the modified tester can directly read the small-signal dynamic transconductance of a FET. To accommodate low-transconductance FETs, the circuit requires that the voltmeter's most sensitive range be no higher than 3 millivolts full scale.

NAND gates U_{1-a} through U_{1-d} form the oscillator section of the test circuit that generates the test signal. This test signal is a square wave with a frequency of 2,500 hertz, whose amplitude is substantially reduced by the voltage divider consisting of resistors R_1 through R_3 and diode D_1. The diode also stabilizes this voltage by reducing any changes that are due to variations in the power supply.

The 5-kilohm potentiometer R_3 is adjusted until the test point shows an output of 10 mV. As a result, the FET under test produces an output voltage across the sampling resistor R_4, which is placed in the drain path of the FET. This output voltage varies at the rate of 1 mV per millimho of the FET transconductance. The same voltmeter as is used to set the test point at 10 mV must also be used to calibrate the transconductance of the FET. The n-channel FET shown in the circuit is only an example, for p-channel FETs can also be easily calibrated by changing the polarities of the gate and the drain supplies. A typical characteristic curve for the FET under test may be plotted that demonstrates the transconductance versus the gate bias. A similar curve for varying drain current can also be plotted. Gate and drain voltages are adjusted by separate power supplies. □

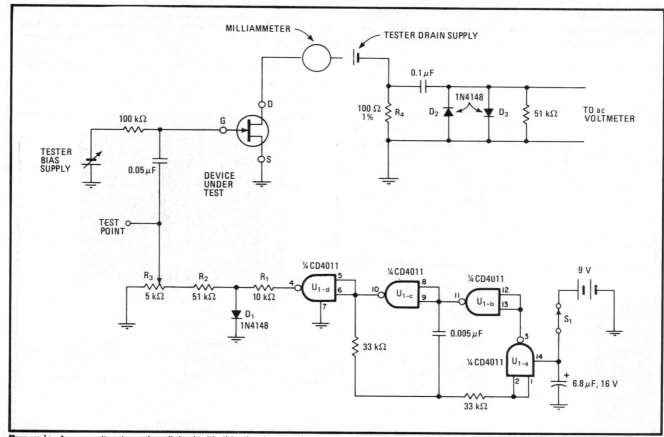

Dynamic. An ac voltmeter, when linked with this simple test circuit, can be calibrated to read directly the dynamic transconductance of an FET. The test signal, generated by NAND gates U_{1-a} through U_{1-d}, is fed into the gate of the FET under test whose output across R_4 is measured by the voltmeter. This output voltage varies at the rate of 1 mV per millimho of FET transconductance.

Versatile circuit measures pulse width accurately

by Kelvin Shih
General Motors Proving Grounds, Milford, Mich.

Designed to measure the width of a pulse, this circuit produces a dc voltage output that corresponds to the input pulse width—from 0.5 to 5.0 volts dc for a 1- to 10-millisecond input pulse width. Among its many potential applications, one of the most attractive is its use in measuring very low frequencies of under 1 hertz accurately and without waiting.

Schmitt trigger U_{1-a}'s output at point A is a pulse of the same width as the input and with a fixed amplitude of 7.5 v (Fig. 1a). The sample-and-hold pulse at point B is generated at the trailing edge of the input. After this signal is shifted in level from 0 to +7.5 v to ±7.5 v, the pulse is used to drive bilateral switch U_{3-b}. The signal at point C is the sum of the width of the input and the sample-and-hold pulse at B and, after level-shifting, resets integrator U_2 to zero when the input is low.

The integrator converts the input into a negative-going linear ramp that remains steady during the brief sample-and-hold period (Fig. 1b). During the rest of the cycle, the capacitor is discharged by U_{3-a} and the output of the integrator stays zero. Inverting amplifier U_4 changes the negative ramp into a positive one. The last stage, which is the sample-and-hold circuit, is used to store the peak

voltage of the ramp, which is proportional to the input pulse width. The output is a constant dc voltage if the pulse width is constant.

In the application for measuring low frequencies, two of the circuits serve as building blocks in a larger circuit that measures the flow rate of a turbine-type flowmeter (Fig. 2). Because of the low frequency involved, a standard counting method takes about 90 seconds to obtain one reading. With the circuit shown, the sampling time is reduced to a fraction of a second. □

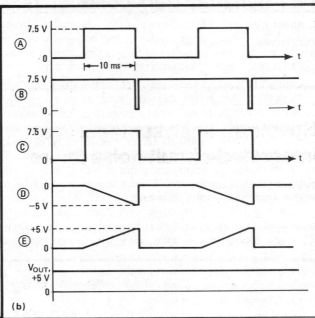

(b)

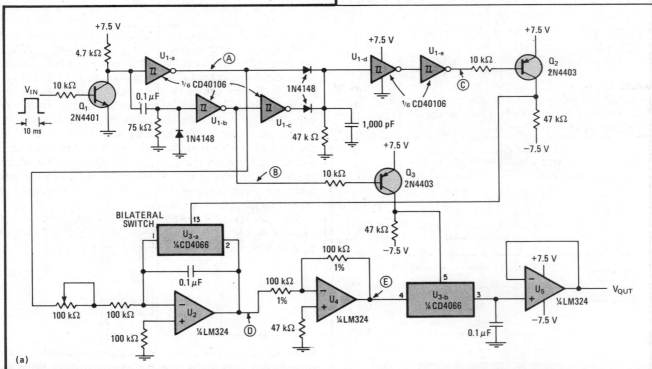

1. Measuring width. This pulse-width–measuring circuit (a) produces a dc voltage output that is proportional to the input pulse width. For the components shown, the output is 5 V dc for a 10-ms input pulse width. Integrator U_2 converts the input pulse width into a linear ramp (b) whose peak voltage is stored in the sample-and-hold circuit. The output voltage is constant if the pulse width is constant.

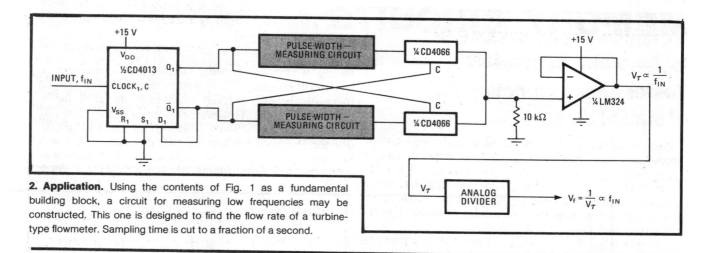

2. Application. Using the contents of Fig. 1 as a fundamental building block, a circuit for measuring low frequencies may be constructed. This one is designed to find the flow rate of a turbine-type flowmeter. Sampling time is cut to a fraction of a second.

Spectrum analyzer measures integrated-circuit noise figure

by Lowell Kongable
Motorola Semiconductor Products Sector, Phoenix, Ariz.

Now that video detectors are incorporated into an amplifier chip containing intermediate-frequency circuitry (MC13001), only the detector output is available, thus making noise-figure measurement difficult. However, a method using a spectrum analyzer eliminates this difficulty. A bonus is that it can test any frequency.

The noise figure of an amplifier is the signal-to-noise ratio at the input divided by the S/N ratio at the output. The noise figure of the device (Fig. 1a) is given by:

$$\frac{(GKTB + P_n)E_g^2/4R_g}{(KTB)GE_g^2/4R_g} = 1 + P_n/GKTB$$

where G = amplifier power gain, P_n = all forms of wide-band noise generated within the amplifier, K = Boltzman's constant, T = temperature (K), and B = amplifier bandwidth (hertz). Because $P_n = V_n^2/R_o$, the noise figure in decibels is:

$$10 \log V_n^2 - 10 \log G - 10 \log KT - 10 \log 1.2 \times B - 10 \log R_o + 1.05$$

A multiplier of about 1.2 is applied to the i-f bandwidth to approximate the equivalent noise-power bandwidth. The compensating factor for the spectrum analyzer is 1.05 dB.

To illustrate this measurement technique, the circuit in Fig. 1b measures the noise figure of Motorola's MC13001. The generator is set at a 43-megahertz carrier that is 30% amplitude-modulated with 10 kilohertz. The spectrum analyzer's center scale is set to 43 MHz and its i-f bandwidth made narrower than the IC's.

To obtain the noise figure of an amplifier, the generator must be connected to the spectrum analyzer and adjusted so that a display amplitude may be easily measured and the setting noted. Next the generator and analyzer are connected to the input and output of the amplifier. In addition, the spectrum analyzer's center scale should be reset to 0 and the generator adjusted so that the display equals the original display. If $R_i = R_g$, the gain may be read in decibels directly from the generator attenuator dial and substituted for 10 logG.

The generator is disconnected and R_g is attached to the amps input so that the root-mean-square noise voltage is displayed on the analyzer. The video filter of the analyzer is narrowed to 0.01 of the i-f band and the rms noise value is measured. The analyzer's i-f bandwidth is measured for accurate results.

For the MC13001 where G = 79 dB, a-m = (10 kHz − 30%), $R_i = R_g$ = 50 ohms, R_o = 100 Ω, T = 298 K, and B = 1,150 Hz, the noise figure is 5.42 dB. □

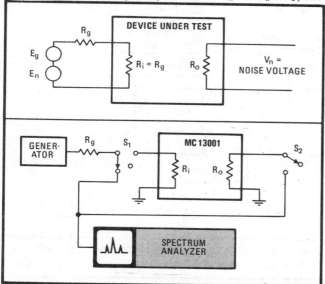

Noise figure. Amplifier's noise figure (a) is determined by the signal-to-noise ratio at the input divided by the S/N ratio at the output. The circuit (b) measures the noise figure of an integrated circuit with a spectrum analyzer. This technique measures the detected low-frequency output of the MC13001.

MEMORY CIRCUITS

Tester checks functionality of static RAMs

by David J. Kramer
Sunnyvale, Calif.

Before a TTL-compatible random-access memory is inserted into boards, it is customarily checked out for functionality with a tester specifically designed for its particular bit size. However, this tester can examine all RAM sizes from 256-by-1-bit on up to 4-K-by-8-bit devices. It detects the bit sites that do not store a 1 or 0, faulty address inputs and buffers, and malfunctioning write or chip-enable inputs. However, it cannot deter-

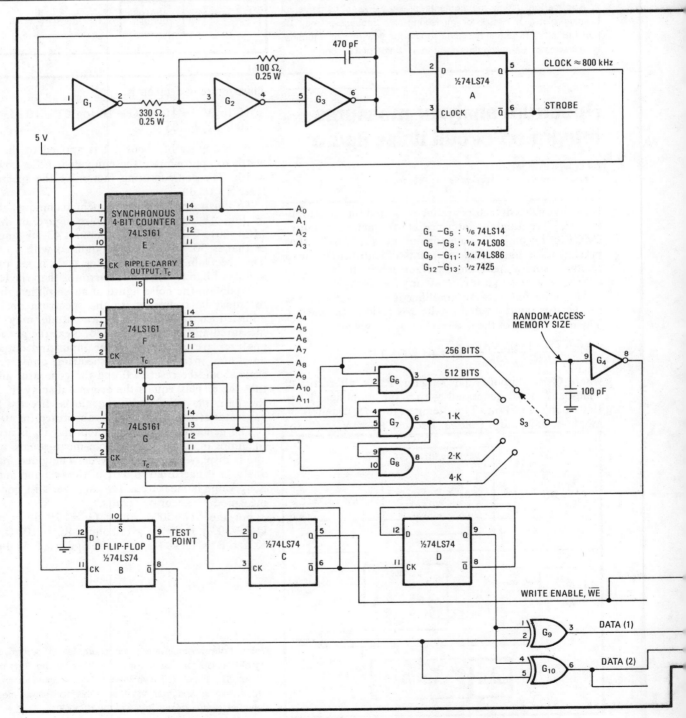

mine excessive supply current, slow timing, or other parametric faults.

The error-detecting circuitry (Fig. 1) basically consists of a clock, counters, a pattern generator, and exclusive-OR gates. Pinouts for bit-wide, nibble-wide, and byte-wide RAMs are shown in Fig. 2a, b, and c, respectively. The clock, composed of inverters G_1 through G_3 and flip-flop A, generates a 800-kilohertz square wave that is fed to counters E, F, and G. The counter outputs cycle through the addresses of the device under test. The pattern generator composed of flip-flops B, C, and D generates the $\overline{WE}$ signal and the data stream.

In each write cycle (Fig. 3) the data written into the bit site of the lowest and highest address is the complement of the data written into all other sites. Consequently, a faulty address buffer and decoder places this data in a site other than the lowest or highest and the error appears in the following read cycle.

The signals at the outputs of exclusive-OR gates J, K, and G are inverted and designated ERR_1, ERR_2, and ERR_3. This inverted ERR signal is fed to the one-shot L that is used as a pulse stretcher. The $\overline{WE}$ and STROBE inputs ensure that the one-shot is enabled only during a read cycle, when the RAM output data is valid. The RAM

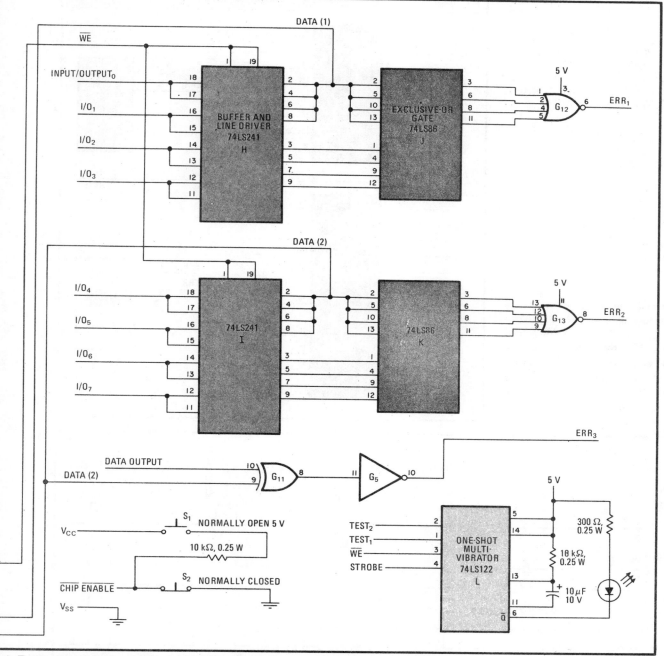

1. Tester. Error-detecting circuitry basically consists of a clock, counters, a pattern generator, and exclusive-OR gates. Inverters G_1 through G_3 and flip-flop A form the clock, which generates a 800-kHz square wave. Flip-flops B, C, and D constitute the pattern generator. Exclusive OR gates J, K, and G_{11} send their inverted ERR signals to one-shot L, used as a pulse stretcher.

2. Package. Pinouts for bit-wide, nibble-wide and byte-wide RAMs are as shown in (a), (b), and (c). The circuit also shows the connections of ERR signals to the appropriate pins of the one-shot L.

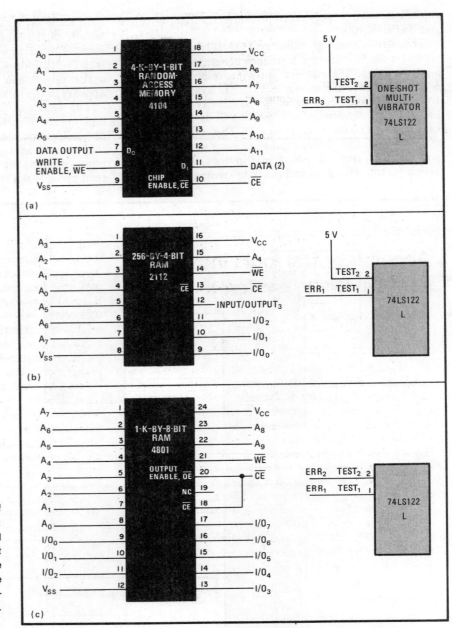

3. Waveforms. One test cycle consists of four test sequences in the following order: write DATA, read DATA, write $\overline{\text{DATA}}$, and read $\overline{\text{DATA}}$. XXF represents the highest address of the RAM under test. In each write cycle, the data written into the bit site of the lowest and highest address is the complement of the data written into all other sites. The Q output of flip-flop B is a test point.

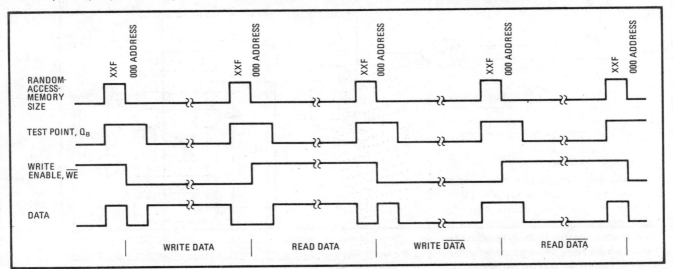

SIZE input of the pattern generator is connected to the appropriate size of the RAM by means of switch S₃.

For example, if a 2-K-by-4-bit RAM is to be tested, the 2-K line is connected to the RAM SIZE input. The ERR₁ line is then connected to the TEST₁ input of one-shot L, while the TEST₂ pin is held high. Finally V_cc, $\overline{WE}$ and $\overline{CE}$ are connected to the appropriate pins of the RAM under test and the tester is now ready for operation.

If a RAM is working properly, the light-emitting diode lights momentarily when S₁, which is normally open, is pressed. However, it stays on or flickers for a bad RAM. The $\overline{CE}$ line is tested by pressing normally closed S₂. If the LED does not light, there is faulty $\overline{CE}$ circuitry in the RAM that is keeping it enabled at all times. In addition, the LED will never light if a short exists between V_cc and V_ss, which pulls down the supply voltage. □

Access control logic improves serial memory systems

by Robert G. Cantarella
Burroughs Corp., Paoli, Pa.

File storage systems used in large scientific processors or computers need serially organized dynamic random-access-memory systems to transfer blocks of data from one memory unit to another in a serial order. Dynamic RAM devices used in such secondary stores need to be refreshed in a fixed cyclic order to keep the cost and latency low. This refresh logic loop further reduces latency, while retaining the cost advantage of a serial organization, and refreshes the memory at twice the minimum rate. In addition, zero latency is guaranteed with block transfers of at least L milliseconds.

When an initial transfer request XFERRQST occurs, the requester's address RQSTADDR is loaded into the refresh counter, which resets the refresh loop. This set-ting initiates the transfer (XFERSTART) with zero latency. The refresh address is then held in the refresh counter. Because the refresh loop is cycling at twice the required frequency, all bits are properly refreshed within L ms. The reset is then enabled only after a full cycle has completed when the time-out down counter is loaded with L ms. However, this action only occurs when the time-out down counter is zero.

After the transfer request is initiated, access is granted either when the requester's address is identical to the refresh address or when the time-out down counter is zero. Thus latency is a function of the requester's address and the time since the last reset. As a result, a block transfer of L ms guarantees that the next transfer request will be granted immediate access.

The system performs like a random-access memory but retains the cost advantages of a serial-memory system. The constant refresh rate results in a steady current drain, thereby reducing the cost of the power-supply system and storage cards. □

Engineer's notebook is a regular feature in *Electronics*. We invite readers to submit original design shortcuts, calculation aids, measurement and test techniques, and other ideas for saving engineering time or cost. We'll pay $75 for each item published.

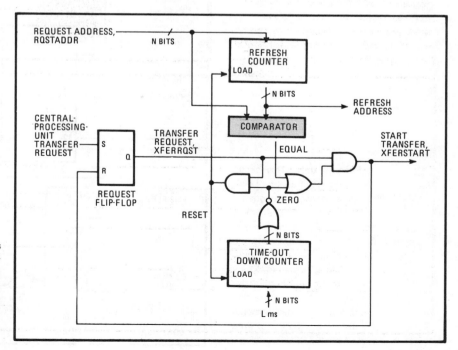

Access. The access control logic refreshes the memory at twice the requisite frequency to keep the latency low. Access is granted when the requester's address is identical to the refresh address or the time-out down counter is zero, whichever occurs first. Block transfer of L ms guarantees zero latency.

Transferring data reliably between core and CPU RAM

by Trung D. Nguyen
Litton Data Systems Division, Van Nuys, Calif.

Magnetic-core memories are still one of the most dependable ways to store large amounts of nonvolatile digital data (up to 1 megabyte). This circuit is a conduit for data transfer between the core memory and the random-access memory situated in the central processing unit. A word in the core is composed of 3 bits and is matched to the RAM's 18-bit words. Because of the low bits-per-word count in core, circuit reliability is high and costs are low.

The data that will be written into or read from core is temporarily stored in the data-register circuit. During the write cycle, input data D_{I/O_1} through $D_{I/O_{18}}$ is loaded into the core write-data register, which is composed of flip-flops U_1 through U_3 (Fig. 1). The two most significant bits—17 and 18—are used as parity bits for low-

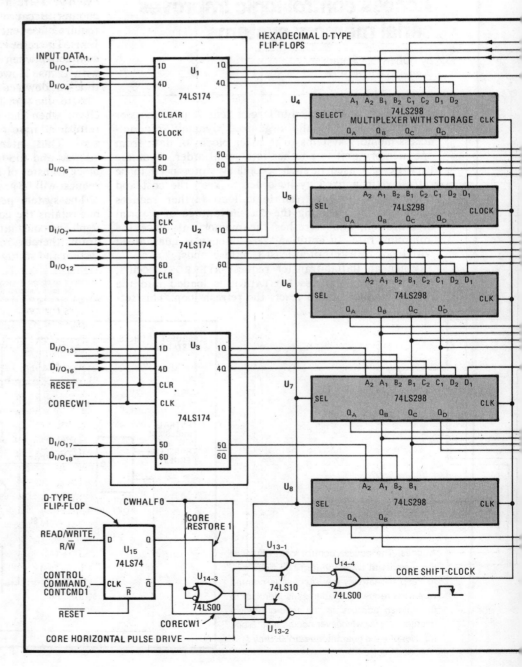

1. Shifting data. This circuit allows two-way transfer of digital data between magnetic-core memory (3 bits/word) and the random-access memory (18 bits/word) located in the central processing unit. Data shifting is controlled by the horizontal pulse-drive signal supplied to the core, and the direction of data transfer is controlled by the read/write pulse from the CPU.

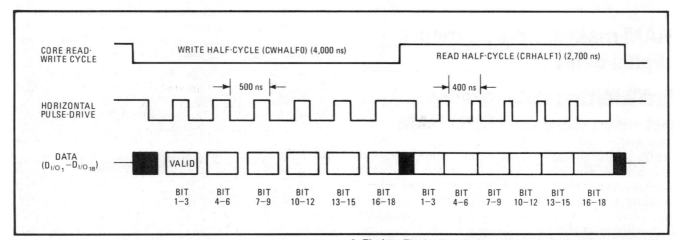

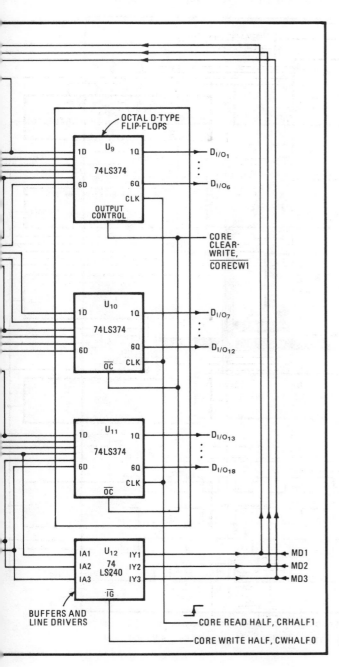

2. Timing. The horizontal drive signal supplied to the core is pulsed six times during each read or write half-cycle to shift data from the core to the RAM and *vice versa*. A typical R/W core-cycle lasts 6.7 microseconds, thereby permitting a data-transfer rate of 150,000 words per second with each word comprising 18 bits.

and high-order data bytes. In addition, on the leading edge of the core clear-write pulse (CORECW1), the data is transferred to the storage-multiplexer circuit, which comprises multiplexers U_4 through U_8. This pulse clears the location of the addressed word in the core memory.

Serial data is sent to the core read-data register (flip-flops U_9 through U_{11}) during the read cycle. This data travels through the storage-multiplexer circuit, which now functions as a data-shift register.

The word-select input is low during the read half-cycle. As a result, a 3-bit word from the core is shifted through the data-shift register by the core's horizontal pulse-drive signal and stored in the core's read-data registers. When the core clear-write pulse is low, this data reaches the RAM. The shift registers are clocked by the shift clock's (CSHIFTCH) negative-going edge, which occurs for every positive-going core horizontal pulse. The horizontal drive signal pulses six times for each memory half-cycle (Fig. 2).

In contrast, during the write half-cycle, the multiplexer word-select input is high and the RAM's 18-bit word is shifted through registers U_4 to U_8 by the horizontal drive pulse and stored in the core's write data register. When the core clear-write pulse is high, the data reaches the core memory.

For proper core-memory operation, the core read/write and horizontal pulse-drive signals are generated by the programmable read-only memory. Data shifting occurs on the leading edge of the core's horizontal drive pulse through its R/W cycle. In addition, the transfer of data during R/W operation is also controlled by NAND gates U_{13-1} and U_{13-2}. The average data-transfer rate per second is 150,000 words, at 18 bits/word. However, if the number of bits per word differs from those mentioned, the horizontal drive pulse, which serves the core module as a timing signal, must be modified. □

RAM makes programmable digital delay circuit

by Darius Vakili
Bayly Engineering, Ajax, Ont., Canada

For applications lacking in long shift registers and for which bipolar components are too expensive, this simple random-access-memory circuit will program the delay of digital signals precisely and accurately—and without needing varying clock frequencies. The RAM's ready availability and low cost add to the circuit's attractions, especially when high signal speeds are involved.

A digital input code programs the output delay of the signal. The input signal is written into the RAM U_1 at an address generated by synchronous up-down counters U_6 and U_7 and by a fixed input digital code set by the dual–in-line–packaged switch. The stored signal is available at the output when the write-enable input to the RAM is high. This data is read out of the RAM from a location that corresponds to the address generated by the counters only. Therefore, the signal read from the RAM is delayed by a time period equal to the DIP switch's displacement value multiplied by the period of the clock used for generating the address.

The input clock is divided by 2 by latch U_9. The Q_2 output of U_9 clocks address counters U_6 and U_7 and also the select inputs of multiplexers U_2 and U_3. The NAND gates generate the RAM's read and write inputs and also ensure the data is written into the RAM when the control input of U_2 and U_3 is high and read out when it is low. □

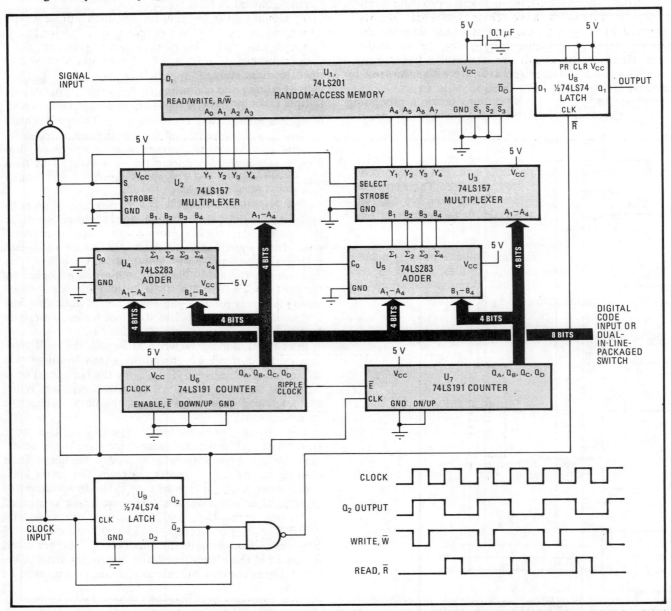

Programmed delay. Using random-access memory, this programmable-delay circuit accurately controls signal delay by means of a digital code generated by a DIP switch. Counters U_6 and U_7 generate the address for the RAM. U_9 provides the write and read inputs for the RAM.

Stepper checks state of E-PROM's memory

by Steven Bennett
Harris Semiconductor, Melbourne, Fla.

Too often, ultraviolet-light–erasable programmable read-only memories have their contents blindly destroyed by users who cannot determine whether the memory contains valuable information or is totally blank. However, this circuit can scan each E-PROM location with a binary counter and so will distinguish memories that contain data from those that do not—all at a cost of around $8.

In use, the memory device is placed into the test socket and the momentary contact switch, S_1, is pressed. If as little as 1 bit of memory is stored in any of the E-PROM's locations (logic 0 for an E-PROM), the light-emitting diode will light.

A 2-kilohertz clock signal for the 12-bit binary counter, B_1, is generated by oscillator and buffer A_1 so that the addresses will cycle through the 2716 2-K-by-8-bit E-PROM in about 1 second. (Although this circuit was dsigned for the 2716, it may also be adapted for any type of memory, bipolar or MOS.)

If any bits in a given location are low, then a pulse will be generated at the E-PROM's output and will drive the 4068 NAND gate high. This pulse, which is generated at the NAND output, is stretched to 2 s by one-shot and buffer A_2 to drive the LED. ☐

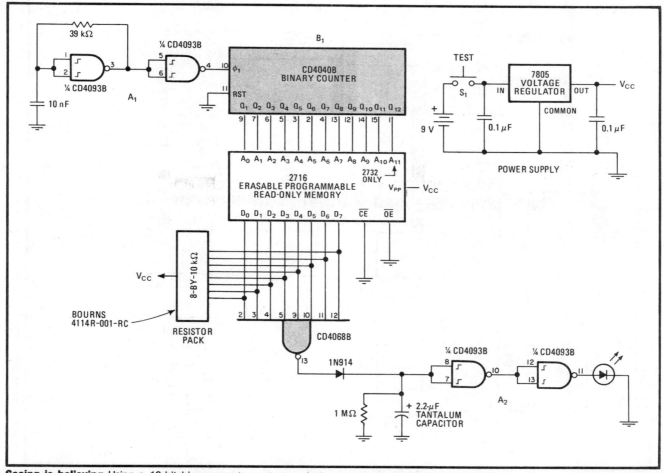

Seeing is believing Using a 12-bit binary counter, a tester of ultraviolet-light–erasable PROMs inspects each location of the device to determine if it contains data or is blank, thereby saving contents from accidental erasure. For a 2-K-by-8-bit E-PROM, the test takes about 1 second, with a light-emitting diode turning on if any memory location contains a data bit.

Random-access memories form E-PROM emulator

by David J. Kramer
Sunnyvale, Calif.

Many low-cost microprocessor kits that are used as educational tools possess a relatively small amount of on-board random-access memory and are incapable of transferring programs to erasable programmable read-only memories. This E-PROM emulator overcomes both of these limitations.

Four 2114 RAMs are connected in a 2-K-by-8-bit configuration (Fig.1). To emulate an E-PROM, this memory

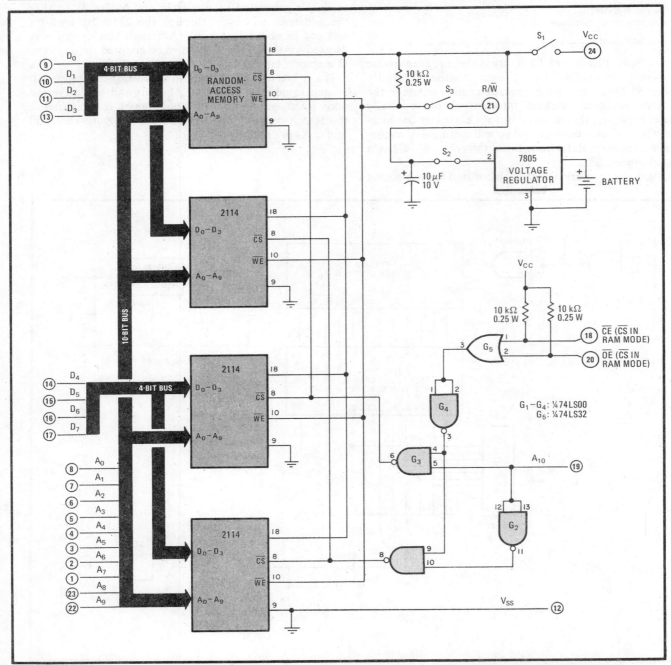

1. Emulator. Four 2114 RAMs are wired on a separate board to simulate a 2-K-by-8-bit E-PROM. Using switches S_1 and S_2, power supply V_{CC} for the emulator can be taken either from a trainer's kit or a battery. Numbers within circles denote pinouts for the 24-pin DIP.

2. Package. The pinouts of the emulator in both its modes—random-access memory and erasable programmable read-only memory—are as shown in (a) and (b). The only differences are in pins 18, 20, 21, and 24—in the E-PROM mode, pins 18 and 20 function as chip and output enable.

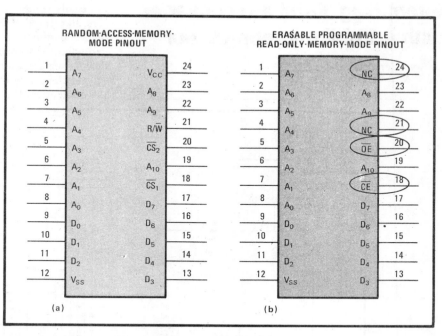

RANDOM-ACCESS-MEMORY-MODE PINOUT

ERASABLE PROGRAMMABLE READ-ONLY-MEMORY-MODE PINOUT

(a)

(b)

circuit is built on a separate board and has its leads terminating in a 24-pin dual in-line package. The power supply for the emulator is either from the microprocessor training kit (V_{cc}) or a battery and is coupled to the emulator by using switches S_1 or S_2. The $\overline{WE}$ line may be disconnected from the plug with S_3.

To function as an emulator, the 24-pin DIP must be connected to the appropriate address-decoding circuitry in the trainer. The memory is then plugged in and either S_1 or S_2 is closed (depending on the selected power supply). This puts the circuit in its RAM mode (Fig. 2a). In this mode, pins 18 and 20 function as chip-select controls. Pin 21 is the read-write input.

Once the data to be preserved is in the RAM, the battery should be (if not already) connected to the 7805 voltage regulator, and S_2 closed and then S_1 and S_3 opened. The circuit is now in its E-PROM mode (Fig.2b) and may be inserted in the master socket of any programmer that will handle a 2716 E-PROM.

The emulator will remain to be powered while the programming occurs. The type of keep-alive battery needed depends on the power requirements of the 2114 RAMs and the length of time the emulator is to remain in the E-PROM mode. □

MICROPROCESSORS

Interfacing 10-bit a-d converter with a 16-bit microprocessor

by Sorin Zarnescu
Westwood, Calif.

Eight-, 10-, and 12-bit analog-to-digital converters cannot easily impart their knowledge to 16-bit microprocessors, like Intel's 8086, because the received output is not in 2's complement form and the sign bit has to be extended. However, a match can be made with this design, which can offer programmable interrupt control. In addition, only one input instruction is needed to read the contents of the a-d converter. As an example, Analog

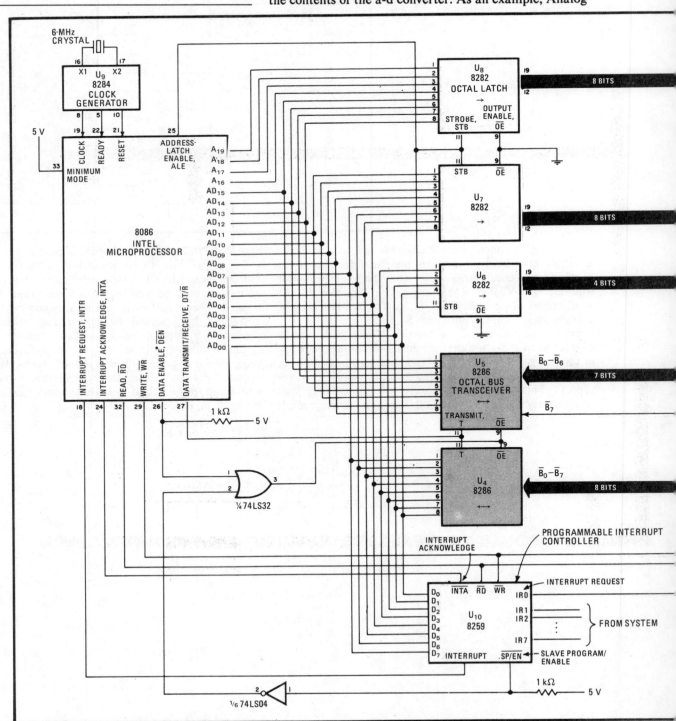

Devices' 10-bit a-d converter, AD571, is used.

Because the a-d converter's output code is offset binary, the most significant bit is inverted and used to control octal line driver-receiver U_3. When the input is positive, the MSB is zero and the octal driver is open. As a result,

seven MSBs are 0. On the other hand, when the input is negative, the octal driver is in its tristate mode and the MSB is 1, resulting in seven MSBs also being 1.

After receiving the data-ready interrupt through programmable interrupt controller U_{10}, the microprocessor

Interface. The circuit provides an easy and fast way to interface Analog Devices' AD571 10-bit a-d converter with Intel's 16-bit 8086. The decode logic provides the a-d converter with signals for reading the data and starting the conversion.

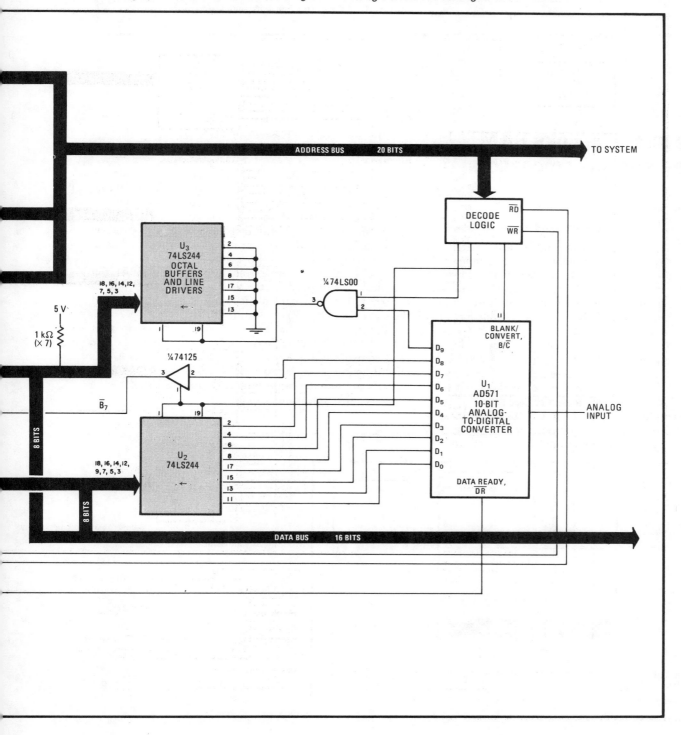

A SEQUENCE FOR THE INTERRUPT ROUTINE		
Mnemonics	Symbolic address	Comments
INP	CONV	; READ DATA
OUT	CONV1	; B/$\overline{C}$ LINE BROUGHT HIGH
⋮	PROCESSING	
OUT	CONV2	; B/$\overline{C}$ LINE BROUGHT LOW (START CONVERSION)
IRET		; RETURN

reads the data through an input command also supplied by U_{10}. Since the 8086 has a multiplexed address and data bus, U_6, U_7, and U_8 are used as latches for the address. In addition, the address-latch–enable output of the processor clocks U_6, U_7, and U_8. Octal bus transceivers U_4 and U_5 provide buffers for the data bus.

The direction of data on this bus is controlled by the data transmit-receive pulse that is generated by the processor. In addition, the data-ready output from the converter is used as an interrupt-request input for U_{10}. The decode logic provides the signals for reading the data and starting the conversion (see table). □

Simple interface links RAM with multiplexed processors

by Jeffrey M. Wilkinson
Harris Semiconductors, Melbourne, Fla.

Normally a sophisticated latch and logic circuitry are required to hook up extra random-access memory to a microprocessor whose memory has run short. However, users wanting to link multiplexed microprocessors with complementary-MOS RAMs will find the assembly much easier and cheaper with this interface, which has only one decoder circuit.

The design takes advantage of the address latches incorporated in the C-MOS RAM used, the Harris HM-6516. Circuit reliability is increased by the reduced parts count, while circuit size and cost along with the application-design time are all also reduced.

As an example, a 2-K-by-8-bit C-MOS static RAM is linked to an Intel 8085A microprocessor. At the start of the memory cycle, the input/output memory control (IO/$\overline{M}$) and the address-latch-enable (ALE) lines move low and the address decoder generates RAM-select. This low-going transition should occur while addresses on the bus are valid.

The decoder's output is fed to the RAM chip-enable pin ($\overline{E}$), which latches the chip's bus address. Address information is then latched in the on-chip address registers by the falling edge of $\overline{E}$. Also, the RAM's address and select inputs should occur simultaneously. After the cycle is complete and the addresses are removed from the bus, a memory read or write cycle occurs.

During the write cycle, the write-control ($\overline{WR}$) pin supplies a write pulse to the write-enable ($\overline{W}$) input on the RAM. The read-control ($\overline{RD}$) pin is held high so that the RAM's output is inactive during this cycle.

The read cycle is similar to the write cycle except that the $\overline{WR}$ line remains high during this interval. The read-control ($\overline{RD}$) line moves low, thus forcing the RAM's output-enable line also to go low. As a result, the RAM outputs are enabled and data can be transferred to the processor through the bus. □

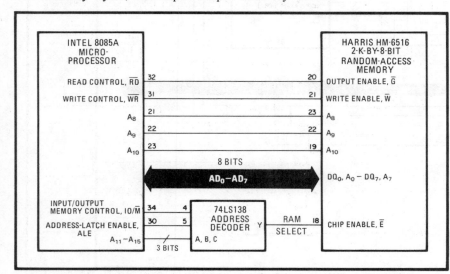

Hook-up. This one–decoder-circuit interface facilitates an easy exchange of data between C-MOS random-access memories having on-chip address latches and multiplexed microprocessors by carefully selecting memory elements that need to be tied to the processor. Circuit assembly time and costs are negligible.

Enabling a processor to interact with peripherals using DMA

by Trung D. Nguyen
Litton Data Systems Division, Van Nuys, Calif.

Most peripheral devices connected to a microcomputer by the peripheral interface bus can request services from the computer over the interrupt line. This facility, though, is lacking on those input/output devices that use

direct memory access to transfer data at high speed between themselves and the processor's main memory. However, a simple interrupt logic circuit will enable such I/O devices to notify the computer when a DMA operation is complete.

As shown in (a), the interrupt-enabling flip-flop U_{1-1} is initially enabled by the enable-service-interrupt ($\overline{ESI}$) command provided by the computer. The computer next sends the external-function-enable ($\overline{EFE}$) command to an addressed I/O device to indicate its readiness for data transfer. If the addressed I/O device chooses to respond to this code, it generates an I/O interrupt request. Interrupt flip-flop U_{2-1} holds this request until the computer

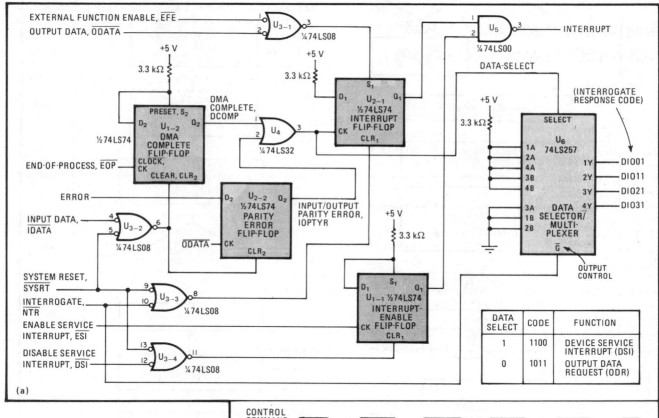

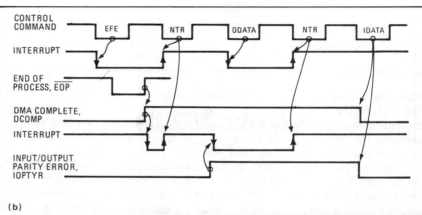

Interrupt. This interrupt logic circuit (a) allows a microcomputer to respond to input/output devices that access its memory directly. The timing diagram (b) of the logic shows that the interrupt line is set when the peripheral device detects an EFE or an output-data command and is reset by the NTR signal. The line is also set by a signal that a direct memory access is complete or that a parity error has been detected.

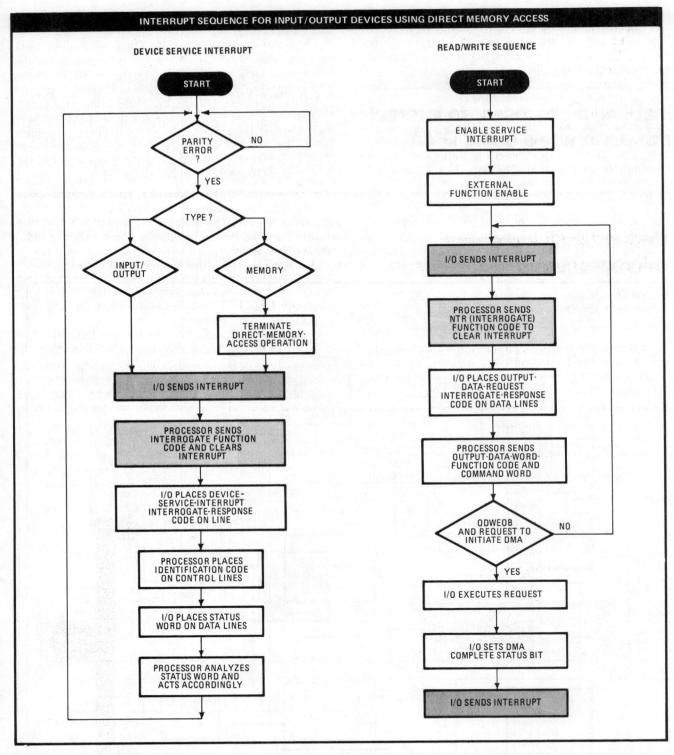

acknowledges it with an interrogate function code.

The I/O device next places the output-data-request interrogate-response code (ODR IRC) on the data lines, whereupon the processor places the output-data-word (ODW) function code and command word on the data lines. Then the I/O device interrupts the processor again for more ODW code, and this procedure continues until all parameters in the command word are sent. The processor indicates completion of the task by sending an output data word with an end-of-block (ODWEOB) signal on the control lines and by requesting the initiation of a DMA operation on the data lines.

Subsequently, the end-of-process (EOP) signal from the DMA indicates that the DMA operation is complete. The I/O device now sets the DMA-complete status bit and issues an interrupt to the processor.

If a memory parity error occurs during the memory-to-memory transfer cycle, the external end-of-process signal (not shown) causes the abrupt completion of the DMA operation and makes the I/O device issue an interrupt. The I/O parity error sets the I/O parity error flip-flop U_{2-2}, which enables the I/O device to generate an interrupt signal (b). The I/O device responds to this parity error interrupt by placing the device-service-interrupt interrogate-response code (DSI IRC) on the data lines. In addition, the processor sends the interrogate command code over the control lines and clears the interrupt. Next, the processor sends the input command code, and the I/O device places the status words on data lines and clears the parity flip-flop. The processor then analyzes the status word and acts accordingly. The table shows the step-by-step interrupt sequence.

The interrupt response codes are generated by data selector–multiplexer U_6. When the processor sends the interrogate ($\overline{\text{NTR}}$) command, U_6 selects either device-service-interrupt (DSI) or output-data-request (ODR) on the basis of the state of the data-select line. If a parity error or DMA completion occurs, the data-select line goes high and DSI is selected. If nothing happens, the data-select line remains low and ODR is selected. The codes for each function are placed on the data line bus, and the processor is programmed to recognize them. □

Redundancy increases microprocessor reliability

by Dan Stern
Stern Engineering, Willowdale, Ont., Canada

A classic way of increasing a microprocessor's reliability is to back it up with an additional identical microprocessor. This circuit generates a pulse to interrupt the processors (or, in this case, microcontrollers) whenever a faulty operation occurs. The pulse then initiates a software recovery routine for changing over to the properly functioning processor.

One-shots U_1 and U_2 continuously monitor the watchdog pulses generated by each microcontroller circuit (see figure). To convert these pulses into logic levels, time constants T_1 and T_2 must be greater than T_{wd1} and T_{wd2}, respectively.

Under normal operation, microcontroller No. 1 is assumed to be the active processor. Therefore when the power is turned on, the active microcontroller produces watchdog pulse T_{wd1} first. As a result, output Q_1 of U_1 is in a high state that prevents one-shot U_2 from being

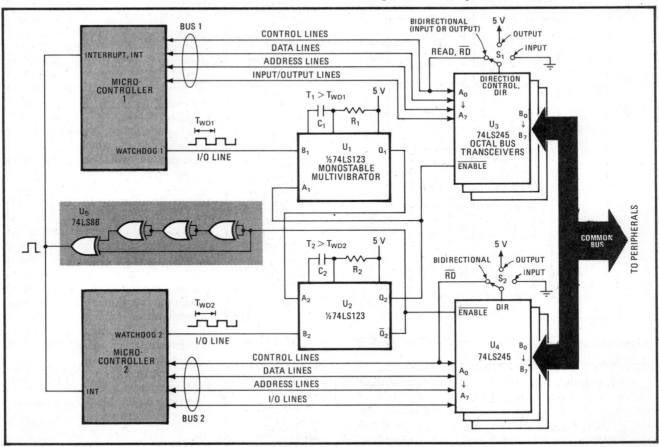

Reliable. Two identical microprocessor circuits are interfaced with a common bus, with microcontroller No. 2 functioning as a back-up circuit in the event of a faulty operation or failure. The watchdog pulses generated by the processors continuously monitor the circuit. When a changeover occurs, U_5 generates a pulse to interrupt the microprocessors and thereby activates a software recovery routine.

triggered. This enables three-state bus driver U_3 and forces U_4 into the three-state mode, thereby connecting bus No. 1 to the common bus.

When microcontroller No. 1 fails to produce a watchdog pulse, Q_1 of U_1 goes low and enables one-shot U_2, which allows watchdog pulse T_{wd2}, generated by the other microcontroller, to trigger U_2. This triggering changes the state of Q_2 to a high logic level, which in turn disables U_3 and switches the common bus to bus No. 2. Simultaneously, a high Q_2 disables U_1 and pre-

vents the common bus from being switched back if unpredictable pulses occur at the first watchdog output.

Every time a changeover occurs, U_5 generates a short pulse to interrupt the microprocessors. As a result, the software recovery routine is activated and ensures a proper changeover to the functional microcontroller.

Each bus may contain as many bus drivers as required, depending on the number of lines per bus. Drivers U_3 and U_4 are switch-selected to operate as input, output, or bidirectionally. □

Octal latches extend bus hold time

by Jim Handy
Intel Corp., Santa Clara, Calif.

Although the timing of microprocessor-generated data and control signals is adequate for most applications,

occasions do arise when the data hold time needs to be extended. Logic-analyzer designs and systems using slow memory or several stages of bus buffering are only two examples of the need for this retention. The simple circuit shown here uses just a chip and a spare gate to increase the data retention time to the entire duration of a bus cycle.

The outputs of the 74LS373 octal latch are each tied to appropriate data bus lines (a). Control signals are derived by combining the read and write signals through OR gate U_2, a function that is required only when the circuit is to be used for logic analysis. In other systems where a slower microprocessor is needed, the write signal alone needs to be connected to the clock and output control pins of the latch.

At reference point A in the timing diagram (b), the read or write signal disables the latch outputs, thereby allowing the data bus to assume the normal mode. The microprocessor or memory device drives the bus, and the clock input is simultaneously actuated. This allows the individual flow-through latches within U_1 to follow the data on the bus.

At time B, when the control signal disappears, the latch's clock signal is removed and the data is held at its last state. Also, U_1's outputs are activated within the delay time of the latch outputs. The total maximum delay of 35 nanoseconds is much smaller than the hold time of most available microprocessors and memory devices. As a result, there are no glitches on the data bus. Data is retained for the entire duration of the bus cycle and is dropped at the occurrence of the leading edge of the next control signal. □

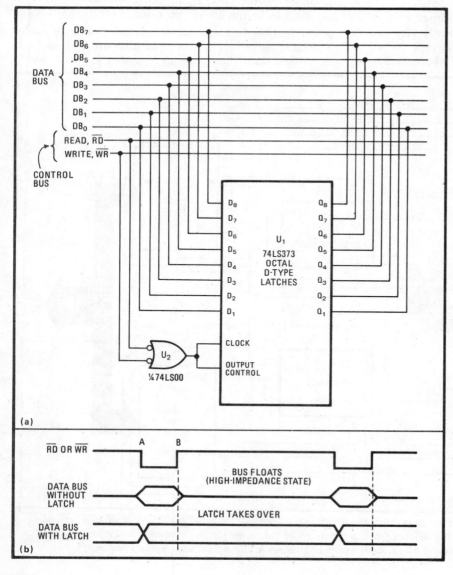

(a)

(b)

Hold on. Using eight latches of the chip 74LS373 and a spare NAND gate wired as a negative-input OR gate, this simple circuit (a) extends the data retention time to the entire duration of a bus cycle. The timing diagram (b) shows that the data is retained until the leading edge of the next control signal is reached.

Single chip solves MC6809 timing problems

by Kim A. Crane
Arizona State University, Mesa, Ariz.

Microprocessor-based systems often have several levels of peripheral decoding. Propagation delays due to these decoding schemes make the bus-timing parameters critical. As a result, they are difficult to keep within specifications from a worst-case–analysis point of view and introduce a timing fault TF.

TF is the amount of time by which the last opportunity to read or write valid data has been missed. However, this configuration uses only one chip and three resistors to eliminate this timing problem for the MC6809 processor when it is being interfaced with either M6800 or non-M6800 family parts.

The circuit (a) takes advantage of quadrature clock Q that is included in the MC6809 chip. The rising edge of this clock indicates that the address bus is valid, and its falling edge indicates that the data bus is valid. In addition, the read-cycle access time is extended by about 250 nanoseconds through enabling the decoders on the

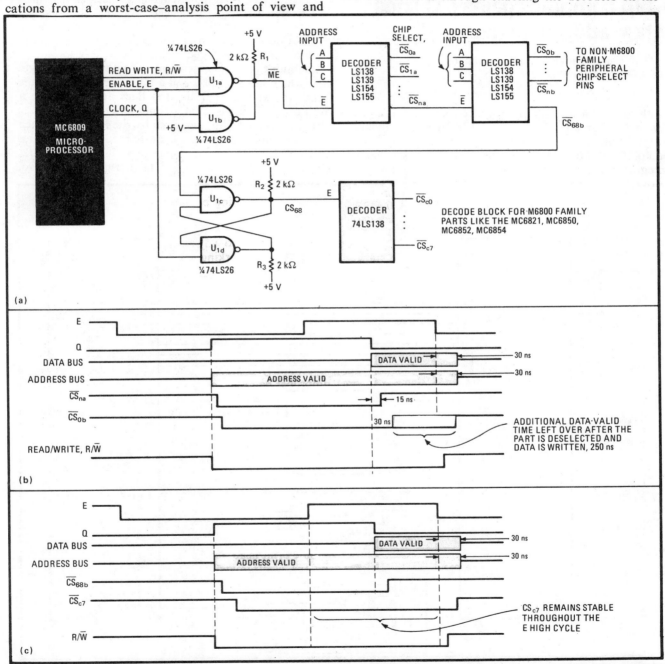

Delay. The circuit (a) ends decoder bus-timing problems on the MC6809 processor when it is being interfaced with M6800 and non-M6800 parts. Diagram (b) shows that a string of 18 74LS138 decoders can be used with this scheme without any timing-delay problems. For interfacing with some M6800 parts, logic extends the chip-select low during a write cycle (c) to the falling edge of E.

rising edge of this clock.

However, the main advantage lies in the write-cycle timing. On the falling edge of Q, during a write-cycle, the decoders that drive the appropriate chip-select high while enable E is only partially through its high cycle are disabled, causing the data to be written. Also, the data is valid until the falling edge of E occurs. This provides the chip-deselect signal with an additional 250 ns to propagate through the various decoding levels and still remain within worst-case timing margins. With this method, no

timing faults will occur for up to 18 levels of LS type decoders connected in series (b).

Unfortunately, this write-cycle technique is not suitable for some M6800 family parts because of the fact that the data is written into these parts on the falling edge of E and not the rising edge of chip-select. Therefore, additional hardware is required for these parts. NAND gates U_{1c} and U_{1d} and resistors R_2 and R_3 solve this problem by extending the chip-select low during a write cycle to the falling edge of·E without affecting the already correct read-cycle timing (c). □

Chip computer gains I/O lines when adding memory

by U. K. Kalyanaramudu and G. Aravanan
Bharat Electronics Ltd., Bangalore, India

With an extended 6800 microprocessor instruction set, 2-K bytes of read-only memory, 128 bytes of random-access memory, and 29 parallel input/output lines, Motorola's 8-bit single-chip microcomputer is a handy integrated circuit for designers to have in their kit.

However, to supplement the MC68701C/6801C's on-chip memory is a complicated matter because I/O lines have to be sacrificed to the need for address and data lines for a memory interface. In this application, though, I/O lines do not have to be surrendered, for the microcomputer unit is interfaced with Intel's 8155-2 RAM.

Combining the microcomputer with the 256-byte RAM, which has I/O ports and a timer, actually gives the circuit an extra 22 parallel I/O lines and throws in a 14-bit programmable counter-timer into the bargain.

Microcomputer U_1's single read-write line is combined with the E clock to provide separate read and write lines as required by RAM U_2—NAND gates U_{4-b} through U_{4-d} help separate the two lines. The I/O-memory control

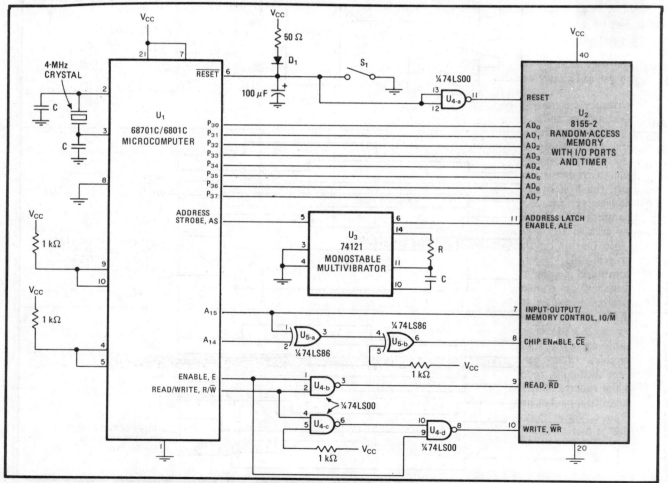

Expansion. Low-cost memory and I/O expansion for the MC68701C/6801C is achieved by interfacing the 8-bit single-chip microcomputer with Intel's 8155-2—a RAM with I/O ports and a timer. The address strobe is trimmed to 200 ns by one-shot U_3 to meet the address setup and hold time requirements of U_2. Read and write signals are generated by gating the E clock.

signal for U_2 is obtained by connecting the line to the most significant address line of the microcomputer, while exclusive-OR gates $U_{5\text{-}a}$ and $U_{5\text{-}b}$ decode the chip-enable from address bits A_{14} and A_{15}. The microcomputer's address strobe is trimmed down to 200 nanoseconds by one-shot U_3 to meet the setup and hold time requirements of 8155-2.

The circuit can also be used for interfacing other peripheral devices, such as the 8755-2, which is an erasable electrically programmable ROM. ☐

Address checker troubleshoots memory drive, logic circuitry

by F. Chitayat
Canadian Marconi Co., Montreal, Quebec

Although error-detecting and -correcting schemes have tremendously enhanced the reliability of microprocessor-based systems, there is still a significant memory failure mode that these schemes cannot detect. If a memory address bit fails due to some problem in the driver or any memory input gate connected to it, the address will be inaccurately written or read. This address checker thoroughly checks for such failures and so complements existing error-correcting schemes. The circuit thus improves the system's troubleshooting capability.

A watchdog monitoring scheme, with the microprocessor programmed to make a certain periodic output that would then be monitored by specialized circuitry, would be only a partial answer, for it would not guard against the failure of more than a few address bits. Instead, the bits checked would generally be only those exercised by the watchdog program. Even if the program ran to 64 locations, at most 6 bits could be checked.

Using this simple circuit, however, the microprocessor clocks the address output onto a register and then reads it back through the data bus. Also, the microprocessor can be programmed to send several test patterns to the circuit by sliding a 1 or a 0 to ensure that every address bit is sent correctly.

The write operation causes the address being written to be stored in registers U_1 and U_2, with the most significant byte stored in U_1 and the least significant byte in U_2. This will not affect the actual writing of the data into the intended address. These registers are read by accessing predetermined memory locations preassigned as input/output locations. In the figure, the specific address locations are referred to as words A and B and are decoded in U_3. When each of these locations is read, the contents of the corresponding register are shifted onto the microprocessor data bus and subsequently read and checked by the microprocessor.

Since a write operation changes the contents of U_1 and U_2, these must be read immediately after a write operation has occurred at the memory-address test location—that is, before another write operation is begun. ☐

Foolproof. This address checker detects faults in memory addresses due to failures in the driver or receiver associated with each address bit. The memory address being written to is stored in registers U_1 and U_2. Since the registers are automatically clocked by a write operation, the error in the memory address is easily detected by the microprocessor when it reads those registers.

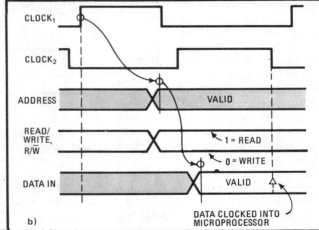

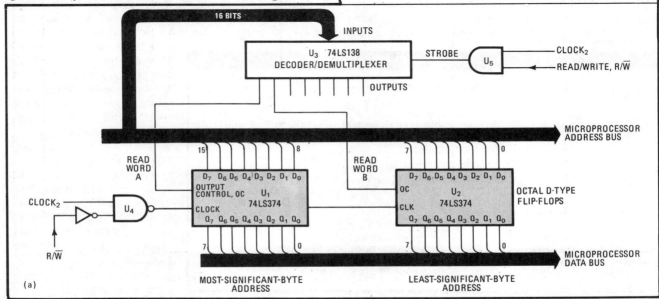

Meter measures processor's dynamic utilization capacity

by Henryk Napiatek
Lacznosci Institute, Gdansk, Poland

An ordinary milliammeter, calibrated in percentages, plays a key role in this simple one-chip, one-transistor indicator of the fractional utilization of a microcomputer's central processing unit in a real-time environment. As a result, the circuit (see figure) will be useful in optimizing system performance and debugging random process routines that typically occur in telephone- and vehicular-traffic applications.

The degree of utilization in processing data and handling interrupts versus the time the machine executes the scheduler's idle loop is simply measured by firing a monostable multivibrator with an output signal derived from the operating system's idle loop. The one-shot's pulse width is set equal to the execution time of the scheduler's idle loop, which generates one pulse for each loop's pass. The scheduler's idle loop is executed only if the processor does not process any data or handle any interrupts. The scheduler's idle-loop execution time is about 50 microseconds. Interrupts cause the processor to execute program routines concerning traffic changes.

The integrated ouput signal of the one-shot thus represents a fraction of the total time the CPU is not being used. This fraction will be indicated by a drop in the reading of the milliammeter that is connected to the inverting output circuit of an npn transistor.

A register-enable pulse or similar signal leaving the output bus of the appropriate system peripheral is applied to the 74123's input. This signal is essentially an idle CPU mark that is derived from the sample idle-loop routine of the scheduler and is written in macro-11 assembly language for the PDP-11/34 minicomputer (see program).

The pulses from the one-shot's output are amplified by transistor Q_1 and integrated by capacitor C_1 and the milliammeter's resistance and distributed inductance. The meter's reading thus reflects the difference between the circuit's 5-volt output limit, which represents 100%

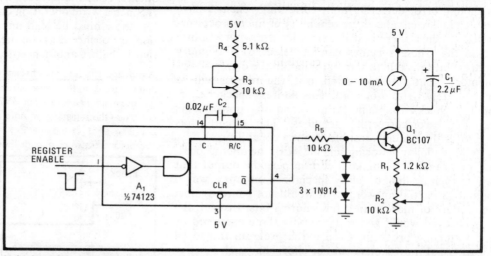

Indexing interrupts. This simple circuit determines the percentage of time the microcomputer's central processing unit is working on processing data and handling interrupts, thus serving as a low-cost optimization and debugging tool. A meter, calibrated directly from 0% to 100%, has typically a 2-μs integration time for rapidly following dynamic changes in machine capacity. The one-shot timer's pulse width is equal to the execution time of the scheduler's idle loop.

CPU utilization, and the total interrupt time, to yield an index of the CPU's actual use.

The circuit is calibrated by adjusting potentiometers R_2 and R_3. To calibrate the meter at full scale, the CPU's idle loop is halted (no input pulses) and R_2 is adjusted for a 100% meter reading. All external interrupts in the idle loop are then disabled (for example, the instruction CLR@#IDLESR should be replaced by the instruction CLR@#LIGHTS) and the routine run. The milliammeter is zeroed by adjusting R_3 for 0% processor utilization. In this case, the processor executes only the scheduler's idle loop. This design can be modified in hardware and software to accommodate indicators other than the milliammeter that can measure other parameters related to real-time operating systems. □

```
            IDLE LOOP OF PDP-11's SCHEDULER USED FOR CIRCUIT CALIBRATION

                    ; ETEXOS W.01/E/.04 OPERATING SYSTEM

         LIGHTS =    177570      ; LIGHTS REGISTER
         IDLESR =    160224      ; REGISTER IN SPECIAL INPUT/OUTPUT DEVICE
         PSW =       177776      ; CENTRAL PROCESSING UNIT STATUS WORD
         PR7 =          340      ; PRIORITY 7
         R3 =            %3       ; CPU'S REGISTER 3
            :
1$:      MOV # PR7+1, @ # PSW     ; EXTERNAL INTERRUPTS DISABLED, BIT C = 1
         MOV # IDLCNT, R3        ; ADDRESS OF IDLCNT 3-WORD VECTOR
         ADC /R3/+              ; BIT C+IDLCNT
         ADC /R3/+              ;
         ADC /R3/+ ·           ;,COUNTING OF IDLE LOOPS IN IDLCNT VECTOR
         CLR @#IDLESR           ; ONE-SHOT TIMER STIMULI
         CLR @#PSW              ; EXTERNAL INTERRUPTS ENABLED
         BR 1$                  ; TO NEXT IDLE LOOP
IDLCNT:  .WORD 0, 0, 0          ; IDLE LOOP VECTOR COUNTER
```

Interfacing C-MOS directly with 6800 and 6500 buses

by Ralph Tenny
George Goode & Associates Inc., Dallas, Texas

Most complementary-MOS devices used with the early members of the 6800 and 6500 microprocessor family are interfaced with the processor bus through programmable interface adapters because bus output data is available for only a short period of time. However, C-MOS devices can be added directly to 6800 and 6500 systems with this circuit. It is assumed some memory-address space is available.

Bus input timing is no problem. It is such that C-MOS latches with output-disable capability can be enabled with an AND/NAND gate of an address-decoding strobe and READ/WRITE signals.

When unassigned blocks of memory-address space exist, C-MOS latches and registers can serve as output registers residing on the processor bus. This technique is demonstrated through a 256-byte block of unused memory that interfaces bus data with a two-character hexadecimal display that is resident on the microprocessor bus (Fig. 1a).

With this design, the high-order address lines are decoded for port selection and the low-order address lines are used to transmit data to that port. Thus the 4-bit binary word is displayed as the equivalent hexadecimal word on the processor bus. The timing information (Fig. 1b) uses worst-case delays associated with C-MOS parts.

Address lines A_4 to A_7 can be decoded through the use of a dual four-input OR gate for U_2 so that a 16-bit output port occupies 256 bytes of memory-address space. The four C-MOS D-type registers U_5 through U_8 use the basic strobe to clock data into the latch (Fig. 2). The four address lines are now used as device enables, so that 4-bit data is entered into one of the four C-MOS parts, resulting in a 16-bit output port. □

2. Expansion. A 16-bit C-MOS parallel output port uses low-order address lines for both data and address. The four C-MOS devices U_5 through U_8 use the strobe to clock the data into the latch. A 16-bit output occupies 256 bytes of address space.

1. C-MOS interface. The logic in (a) allows a C-MOS latch to reside directly on the 6800 and 6500 microprocessor buses. It uses unassigned memory-address space to mix address and data information for a port residing on the processor bus. The bus timing (b) shows that microprocessor data is available for a very short time.

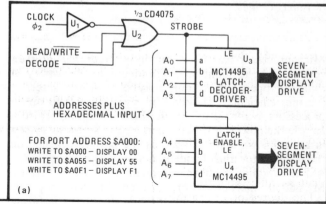

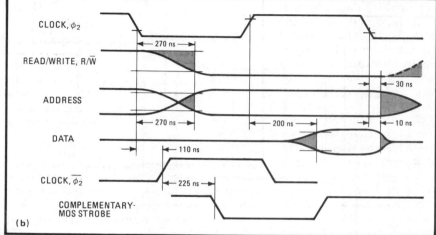

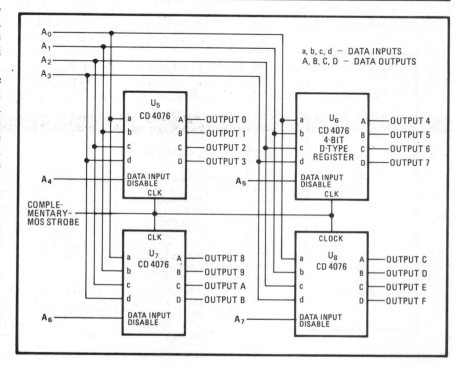

Mapping an alterable reset vector for the MC68000

by Ron L. Cates
Motorola Semiconductor Products Sector, Phoenix, Ariz.

Microprocessor-based system design requires interrupt vectors to be resident in the random-access memory, so that the operating system may control the interrupt routines efficiently. However, many of the 16-bit microprocessors available today use the interrupt structure to handle the power-on-reset function. But since the RAM is in an unknown state as soon as the power is turned on, the reset vector must reside in nonvolatile storage.

The classic solution, implemented here for the MC68000 microprocessor, is a circuit that maps the reset vector for the processor when the power is turned

on and then helps the processor relocate the vector from read-only memory to RAM. But this circuit in fact does more—it also lets the operating system change the location of the reset vector if necessary.

The processor uses addresses 000000 to 000007 to fetch the initial values for the stack pointer and the program counter. The interrupt vectors reside at hexadecimal addresses 000008 to 0003FF. The B part of dual timing circuit U_2 generates a 0.110-second reset pulse when the power supply stabilizes. This positive pulse is inverted and is used to drive the halt and reset inputs of processor U_1 (see figure). When the reset pulse is removed, U_1 reads the first four locations in memory.

Shift register U_3 is cleared only by the power-on-reset condition and is clocked by the address strobe of the processor. The first four memory cycles are mapped into the read-only area of memory. During these cycles, U_3 provides chip-select inputs for both ROM and RAM. The read-write pulse to RAM is inverted by U_4. This lets the processor read the data from ROM while simultaneously

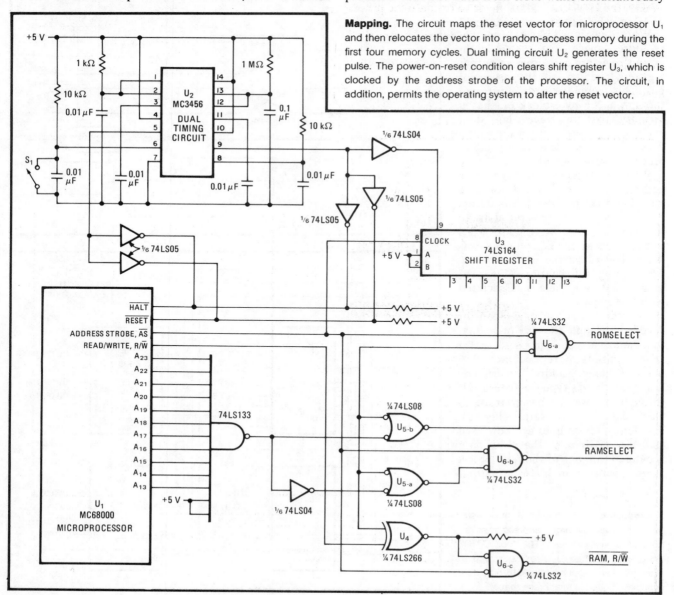

Mapping. The circuit maps the reset vector for microprocessor U_1 and then relocates the vector into random-access memory during the first four memory cycles. Dual timing circuit U_2 generates the reset pulse. The power-on-reset condition clears shift register U_3, which is clocked by the address strobe of the processor. The circuit, in addition, permits the operating system to alter the reset vector.

writing it into RAM locations 000000 to 000007.

When the first four memory cycles are over, U_3 goes into the high state and the decoding occurs. The other half of U_2 furnishes a switch-reset pulse when the system has stabilized. This 11-microsecond pulse sets the processor but does not clear the register. Thus, for all reset conditions set by the U_2-based switch, the vectors must be fetched from the RAM, thereby allowing the operating system to alter them. □

HP64000 emulates MC6801/6803 using bidirectional multiplexer

by M. F. Smith
Department of Computer Science, University of Reading, Reading, England

Because Motorola's MC6801 and 6803 single-chip, 8-bit microcomputers have a multiplexed address and data bus, they are not compatible with MC6800 hardware and therefore cannot exploit the 6800 in-circuit emulation available on the HP64000 development system. However, with the aid of a two-chip bidirectional multiplexer, the HP64000 can be made to emulate the processor portion of these nearly identical chips.

The devices are attractive for a wide range of applica-

Emulation circuit. The circuit (a) allows the HP64000 to emulate the microprocessor portion of both the MC6801 and 6803 by using a converter board that is connected to the HP64212A emulator probe. The bidirectional multiplexer (b) combines the nonmultiplexed address and data lines of the MC6800 emulator.

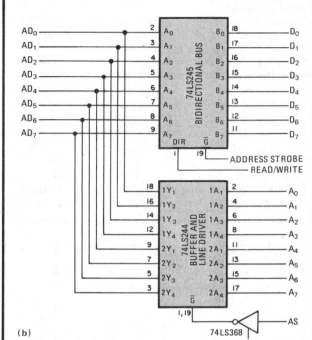

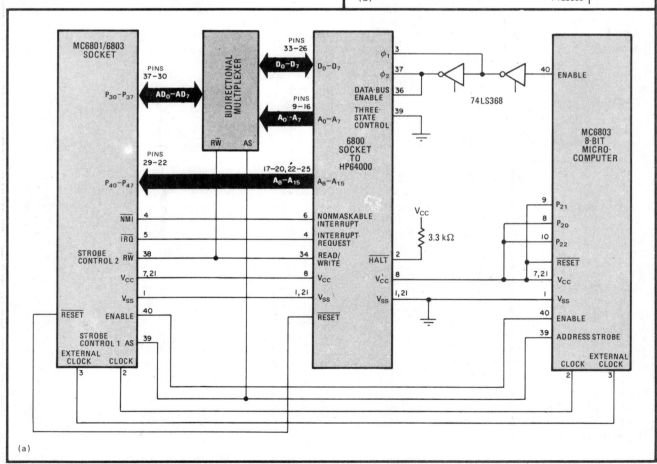

tions, particularly with Hitachi's recent introduction of a complementary-MOS version of the 6801. Besides having complete source and object compatibility with the 6800 software, they have extra instructions for 16-bit operations, an 8-bit multiply, and an X: = X + B instruction, not to mention PSHX/PULX. The units are about 20% faster than the 6800 at the same clock speed.

The circuit (a) allows the HP64000 development system to emulate the microprocessor portion of both the 6801 and 6803 by using a converter board that is connected to the HP64212A emulator probe. The bidirectional multiplexer (b) combines the nonmultiplexed address and data lines of the MC6800 emulator. An address strobe is derived by using a dummy 6801 or 6803 as a clock generator. The circuit allows only the expanded multiplied mode to be emulated. Thus it is not possible to emulate the random-access memory or the input and output of the 6801 or 6803 with this circuit. The assembler of the HP64000 for the 6800 allows use of the extended instruction set of the MC6801/6803. □

8-bit DMA controller handles 16-bit data transfers

by Trung D. Nguyen
Litton Data Systems Division, Van Nuys, Calif.

Many microcomputer systems today are 16 bits wide. But only 8-bit controllers are available to handle direct memory access for them should they need it. This circuit interfaces an 8-bit DMA controller (like a AM9517) with a 16-bit system bus.

As the figure shows in (a), a data strobe loads the contents of an 8-bit data bus into latch 74LS373, and the address enable moves that data onto the address bus. The four least significant bidirectional address lines are inputs from the system data bus (D_8 through D_{11}) when the direct-memory-access controller is idle and are outputs when it is active. The controller's data bus is enabled to input data from D_0 through D_7 during input/output direct-memory-access write, allowing the

processor to program the DMA control register.

The circuit (b) allows the 8-bit controller to transfer data between several 1-megaword core-memory storage modules and a 16-bit system bus. Initially, the outputs of counters A_5 and A_6 are reset to all 0s by the reset line. The A inputs selected by multiplexer A_7 are decoded by A_8 to select a desired module when the module select signal (MSMSELO) is active. Data (not shown) is stored at the addressed location selected by controller's address lines (AD_0 through AD_{15}). The busy signal (MSMBUSY) switches to the busy state when the controller initiates either the reading of data (MEMRO) from the storage

Data transfer. The circuit (a) interfaces the 8-bit DMA controller Am9517 with a 16-bit bus. The register 74LS373 is used for latching an 8-bit controller data bus to complete the 16 bits of the address bus. The four LSBs of the high-order system data bus are used to program the DMA control register. The logic (b) allows the 8-bit controller to handle data transfer of several 1-megaword modules.

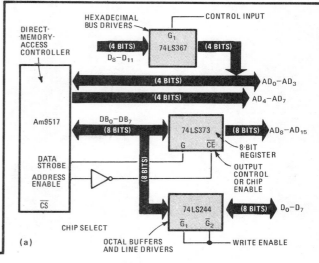

(a)

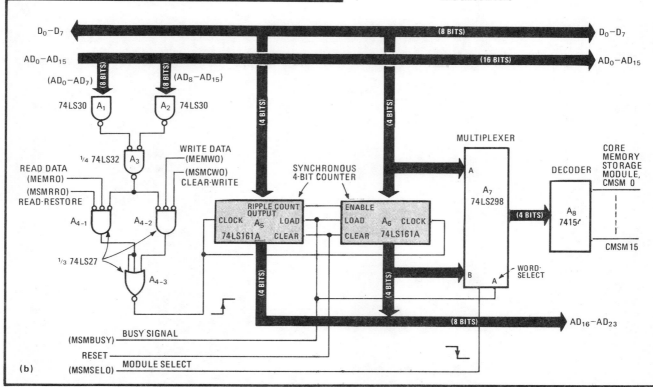

(b)

module during a read-restore (MSMRRO) or writing of data (MEMWO) into the storage module during a clear-write (MSMCWO).

If an address location larger than 64-K is needed to access the storage module, the controller's addresses AD_0–AD_{15} are all high, causing the gate A_3 output to go low. The leading edge of the A_4–A_3 output advances counter A_5 whose output (AD_{16} through AD_{19}) together with AD_0 through AD_{15} is used to access the entire 1-megabit address of the module.

If more than a 1-Mb address location is required, the ripple count output of A_5 goes high, enabling counter A_6 to select the next–higher-order module. The outputs AD_{20}–AD_{23} of A_6 are used for higher address locations. Decoder A_8 selects up to 16 modules. Extra counters and decoders may be added for more modules. □

MODUILATORS & DEMODULATORS

Phase compensation stabilizes pulse-width–modulator system

by Christopher S. Tocci
Clarkson College of Technology, Potsdam, N. Y.

Unlike conventional modulation circuits, this phase-compensated pulse-width modulator employs negative feedback to improve system linearity under varying load conditions—without adding excessive cost to the system. This technique may be used when the average value of the modulator's output is the controlled variable.

The system (Fig. 1) produces a pulse-width–modulated form from an analog input by using a converter to make a differential comparison of that input and a triangular waveform. This information is fed into a fast switching comparator (power driver) having a small amount of hysteresis. The output then feeds back through the phase-shift network comprising a low-pass filter and phase compensator (an all-pass filter).

The phase-shifting properties of the filters and the feedback are shown in Fig. 2. A net phase shift of 180° indicates that together the low- and all-pass filters form an inverting amplifier in·terms of the averaged output

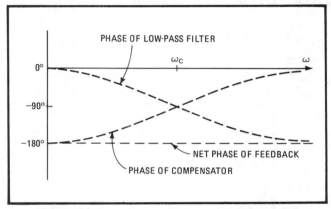

2. Phase. The figure shows the individual phase versus frequency characteristics of a second-order low-pass filter, first-order phase compensator, and the feedback network. The feedback network provides a constant 180° phase shift with respect to the input.

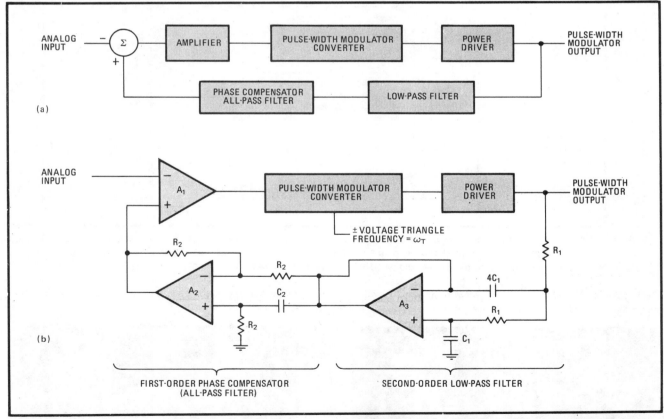

1. Stable. A phase-compensation technique (a) used in this system provides negative feedback and enhances system stability under varying load conditions. Hardware implementation of the system (b) uses a second-order Butterworth low-pass filter and a first-order phase compensator for a constant 180° phase shift of the feedback information.

with respect to the input analog signal.

The low-pass filter by itself must be an even-order part to obtain a constant 180° phase difference with respect to the input. If the amplifier has the typical first-order roll-off at 10 hertz (LM741), then the net phase differential will approach −90° at the summing input with respect to the feedback.

The filters have equal cutoff frequencies. If the switching frequency ω_T is suppressed by 40 decibels ($\omega_C \approx \omega_T/10$), the circuit's feedback error is reduced. □

Linear one-chip modulator eases TV circuit design

by Ben Scott and Marty Bergan
Motorola Semiconductor Products Sector, Phoenix, Ariz.

The fact that Motorola's MC1374 chip has both frequency- and amplitude-modulation and oscillator functions simplifies the design of a television modulator. The device is ideally suited for applications using separate audio and composite video signals that need to be converted into a high-quality very high-frequency TV signal.

The a-m system (Fig.1a) of the 1374 is a basic multiplier combined with an integral balanced oscillator that is capable of operating at a frequency of over 100 megahertz. The fm oscillator-modulator (Fig.1b) is a voltage-controlled oscillator that exhibits a nearly linear output-frequency versus input-voltage characteristic.

This characteristic provides a good fm source with

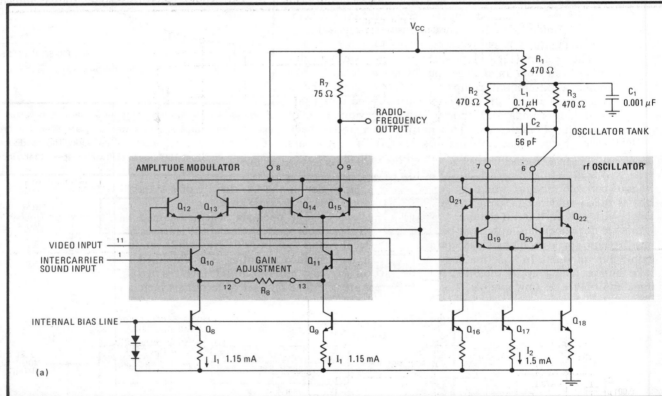

1. Modulator. An a-m (a) and fm (b) modulator and oscillator are incorporated in the design of MC1374. The complete TV modulator circuit (c) uses a simple low-loss second harmonic output filter. Gain resistor R_8 is 2.2 kΩ for an intended video input of about 1 V peak at sync tip. With a 12-V regulated supply there is less than a 10-kHz shift of rf carrier frequency from 0° to 50°C for any video input level.

2. Performance. The IRE test signal (shown at left) is used to evaluate the video modulator. The resulting modulated rf output (shown at right) from the MC1374 has a differential phase error of less than 2° and a differential gain distortion of 5% to 7%.

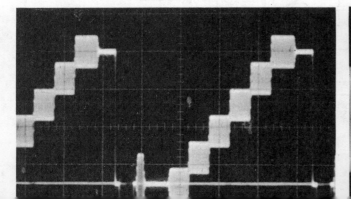
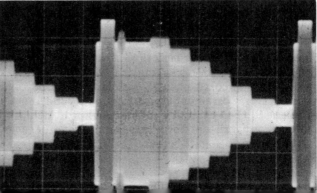

only a few inexpensive parts (no varactor is necessary). The system has a frequency range of 1.4 to 14 MHz and can produce a ±25-kilohertz–modulated 4.5-MHz signal with only 0.6% total harmonic distortion.

The a-m output for a complete TV-modulator circuit (Fig.1c) is taken at pin 9 through a double-pi low-pass filter with the load (R_7 = 75 ohms) connected across pins 8 and 9. Access to both (video and audio) inputs enables the designer to separate video and intercarrier sound sources.

The gain-adjustment resistor (R_8) is chosen in accordance with the available video amplitude. By making $R_8 \cong 2$ (peak video) volts/1.15 milliamperes, a low-level 920-kHz beat is ensured. To keep the background noise at least 60 decibels below the standard white carrier level, the minimum peak video should be at least 0.25 v.

An oscillator for channels 3 and 4 (61.25 and 67.25 MHz) uses a parallel LC combination from pin 6 to pin 7. For this configuration, the value of coil L_1 is kept small and the capacitance large to minimize the variation due to the capacitance of the MC1374 chip (approximately 4 picofarads).

Sloppy wiring and poor component placement around pins 1 and 11 may cause as much as a 300-kHz shift in carrier frequency (at 67 MHz) over the video input range. This frequency shift is due to transmission of the output radio frequency to components and wiring on the input pins. A careful layout keeps this shift below 10 kHz. The video signal and the corresponding modulated rf output (Fig. 2) have a differential phase error of less than 2° and differential gain distortions of 5% to 7%.

The fm system is designed specifically for the TV intercarrier frequency of 4.5 MHz for the U.S. and 5.5 MHz for Europe. The fm system's output from pin 2 is high in harmonic content, so instead is taken from pin 3. This choice sacrifices some source impedance but

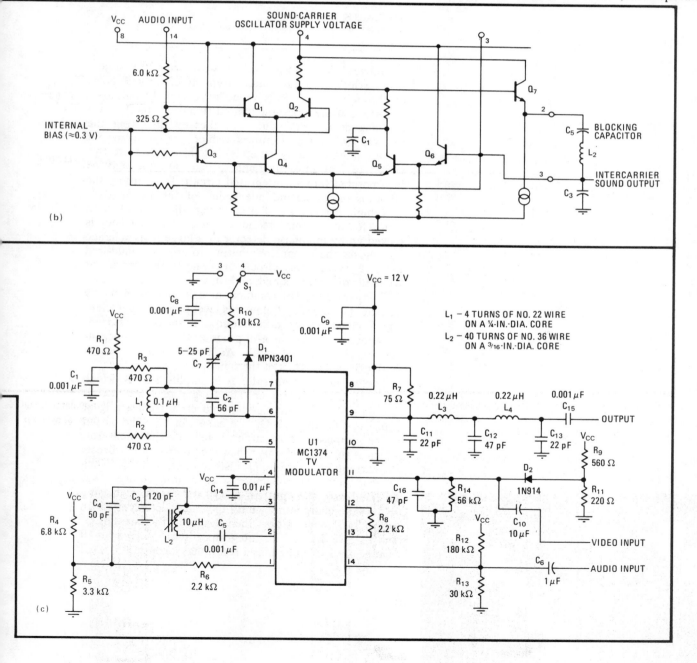

produces a clean fundamental output, with harmonics decreased by more than 40 dB.

The center frequency of the oscillator has approximately the same resonance as L_2 and the effective capacitance from pin 3 to ground. In addition, by keeping the reactance of the inductor at a point between 300 and 1,000 Ω, the overall stability of the oscillator is ensured.

Optional biasing of the audio-input pin (14) at 2.6 to 2.7 v dc reduces harmonic distortion by about 2 to 1. A separate oscillator power supply (pin 4) permits the sound system to be disabled while the a-m section is being aligned.

The modulator circuit has channel 3 and 4 band-switching, video synchronous tip clamping, and audio biasing to reduce distortion further. The value of R_6 permits the intercarrier amplitude to be adjusted easily with the minimum of rf oscillator coupling to pin 1. With a 12-v regulated power supply, there is less than ± 10-kHz shift of rf carrier frequency from 0° to 50°C for any video input level. □

Angle-modulated signals suffer less a-m distortion

by Lowell S. Kongable
Motorola Semiconductor Products Sector, Phoenix, Ariz.

Frequency- or phase-modulated waveforms are subject to a carrier's amplitude modulation either through noise or through the system's modulating signal. This a-m distortion of the angle-modulated signal results in interruptions during demodulation, thereby distorting the received waveform. Limiters reduce the problem but cannot handle highly irregular signals. However, this circuit (a) substantially reduces distortion and may be incorporated into an integrated circuit. In addition, the circuit is automatic and independent of signal strength.

A high percentage of a-m waves allows insufficient signal for fm or pm detection. Instead, the deficiency is picked up by the phase detector as a large phase change and causes the integrator's output to emit an undesired noise. However, this circuit disconnects the integrator while the distortion is high and thus gets rid of the noise.

Comparator A (b) conducts at a level that is set by threshold voltage V_t. Below this level there is insufficient signal for phase detection. In addition, the direct-current voltage supplied by the a-m product detector is independent of the signal strength. As a result, the threshold voltage is independent of the signal.

The output of comparator A is amplified by B, which drives the Schmitt trigger. The trigger generates a control pulse for the sample-and-hold circuit consisting of transistors Q_1 through Q_6 and capacitor C_1. The output of the sample-and-hold circuit is fed into the integrator, which is interrupted only when the control pulse directs the current from Q_3 into Q_9 instead of Q_1 and Q_2. When Q_9 conducts, its collector is at a low voltage that reverse-biases the emitters of Q_1 and Q_2. This biasing retains the charge on C_1 until Q_1 and Q_2 conduct. With nearly 100% modulation, the voltages at the bases of Q_1 and Q_2 are large. The integrator "sees" only a small change at its input and, as a result, has no output. □

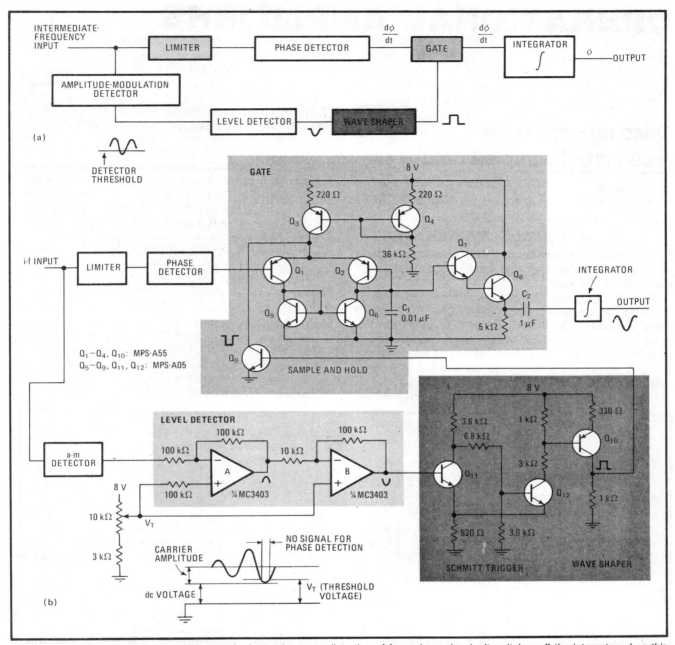

Uninterrupted. The circuit (a) provides a method to reduce a-m distortion of fm and pm signals. It switches off the integrator when this distortion is high (about 100% a-m) and obviates any interruptions in the system. The level detector, wave shaper, and gate are shown in (b).

OPERATIONAL AMPLIFIERS

Quad op amp helps reconstruct sampled data

by Kamil Kraus
Rokycany, Czechoslovakia

Analog waveforms for digital data systems may be reconstructed with this signal processor. It uses a quad operational amplifier that serves both as a sample-and-hold module and filter.

Transistors Q_1 and Q_2, and operational amplifier A_1 make up the sample-and-hold circuit shown. Its input is TTL-compatible. The low-ripple (<0.5 decibel), fifth-order elliptical filter that follows recovers the analog waveform. The passband insertion loss is less than 0.5 dB, and the circuit's stop-band attenuation is greater than 55 dB. A standard communications bandwidth of 3.4 kilohertz is achieved by using a sampling frequency of 8 kHz and a popular elliptical (Cauer) low-pass filter.

Op amps A_2 to A_4 depict the practical implementation of two twin-T networks and an integrator, which comprise the elliptical filter. The normalized transfer function of a single twin-T network is given by $F_1(s) = k_1(s^2+d)/(s^2+bs+a)$ where k_1, a, b, and d are constants that are related to the filter's component values by $d = 1/c_1^2$, $a = 1/c_1^2(1+2m)$, $b = 2(2+m-k)/c_1(1+2m)$, $m = c/c_1$, $k = (R_2+R_3)/R_2$, $k_1 = k/(1+2m)$, c and c_1 are normalized capacitances, and R_1 whose value is 10 kilohms is normalized to equal 1 ohm. Thus, the normalized transfer function of this entire filter is:

$$F(s) = \frac{-17.6(s^2+1/0.02)(s^2+1/0.06)}{(s^2+0.32s+1.27)(s^2+1.01s+0.83)(s+0.70)}$$

and it may be varied by appropriately selecting filter elements. Practical values of C_1 may be obtained from $C_1 = c_1/2\pi f_p R_1$, where f_p is the cutoff frequency.

The overall gain of the circuit is 17.6. The circuit's sample-and-hold will track a 5-volt input signal at 0.5 V/microsecond and hold the signal for up to 100 μs. □

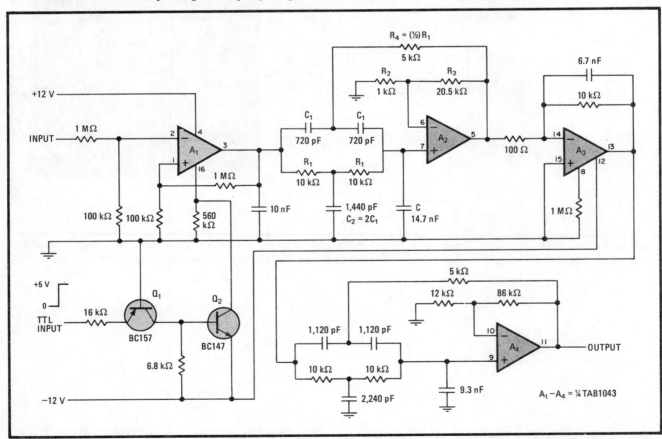

Recovery. This simple circuit built with one operational-amplifier chip derives analog information from its 8-kHz digital-equivalent input. An elliptical filter employed to recover the waveform in a 3.4-kHz baseband uses two symmetrical twin-T networks and an integrator whose characteristics may be varied by selecting the appropriate filter elements. The unit costs around $5.

Bi-FETs expand applications for general-purpose op amps

by Jim Williams
National Semiconductor Corp., Santa Clara, Calif.

With their excellent low-power consumption and low drift, bipolar field-effect-transistor operational amplifiers easily outperform general-purpose (741-type) op amps in a variety of applications [*Electronics*, Nov. 3, 1981, p. 134]. A low-power voltage-to-frequency converter, a battery-powered strip-chart preamplifier, and a high-efficiency crystal-oven controller can also benefit from those qualities of the 441 op amp.

The voltage-to-frequency converter (Fig. 1a) provides linearity to within 1% over the range of 1 hertz to 1 kilohertz. What is more, it does not need an integrator-resetting network using an FET switch, and its current drain is only 1 milliampere.

Integrator A_1 generates a ramp whose slope is proportional to the current into the amplifier's summing junc-

tion. The ramp's amplitude is then compared with the 1.2-volt reference at A_2, which serves as a current-summing comparator.

When the instantaneous amplitude of the ramp exceeds -1.2 v, A_2's output goes low, thereby pulling current from A_1's summing junction. This pulling, aided by diode D_1, causes A_1's output to drop quickly to zero. D_2 biases A_1's noninverting input, providing temperature compensation for the amplifier. These diodes and D_3 are 1N4148 parts.

The 2-picofarad capacitor at A_2 ensures that the output of the amplifier will remain high long enough to completely discharge the 0.01-microfarad capacitor at A_1, thus doing the job of the integrator-reset mechanism. As for calibration, the output is easily adjusted with the 1-megohm potentiometer for a 1-kHz output that is given an input voltage of 10 v.

The 441's low-bias current and its low-power consumption can also yield a simple and flexible preamplifier for strip-chart recorders (Fig. 1b). The circuit is powered by two standard 9-v batteries and may be plugged directly into the recorder's input. As a result, common-mode and ground-loop difficulties are minimized. The gain is variable from 1 to 100, and the time

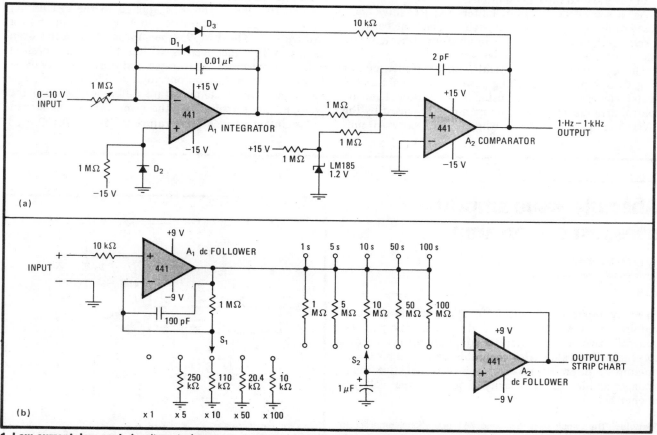

1. Low current, low cost. A voltage-to-frequency converter and preamplifier for strip-chart recorders may be built with the 441 bi-FET op amp. Converter (a), which is easily reset by a capacitor at A_2, provides linearity within 1% over a 0-to-1-kilohertz range and draws only 1 milliampere. A battery-powered preamplifier (b) has an adjustable gain and time constant. The circuit draws less than 500 microamperes.

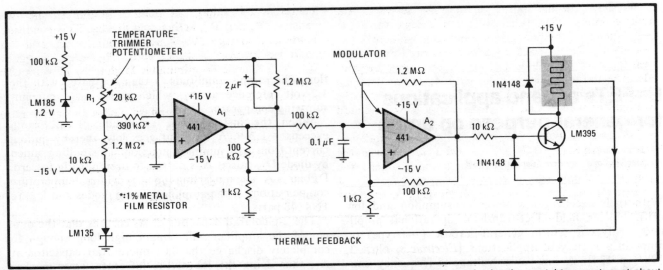

2. Heat switch. This feedback-type controller, using a switching modulator to conserve power, maintains the crystal temperature at about 75°C. Temperature, which may be trimmed over a 4° C range with potentiometer R₁, can be held to within ±0.1°C for a long time.

constant is adjustable from 1 to 100 seconds.

Input amplifier A₁ operates as a dc follower with gain. The gain has five ranges and is selected by S₁. The operational amplifier's input impedance is extremely high (10^{12} ohms) and consequently bias-current loading at the input is around 50 picoamperes. The 10-kilohm resistor in the input line provides current limiting under fault (overloaded input) conditions.

A₂, a second dc follower, buffers the RC filter composed of five resistors and a capacitor. The time constant is selected by switch S₂. This circuit draws less than 500 microamperes, ensuring long battery life.

The efficiency of the crystal-oven controller circuit (Fig. 2) is improved by having power switched across the heater element, instead of using a conventional linear-control arrangement. Oven temperature is sensed by the LM135 temperature sensor, whose output varies 10 mil-

livolts/°C; thus its output will be 2.98 v at 25°C. This signal, converted into current as it flows through the 1.2-MΩ resistor, is then summed with a current derived from the LM185 voltage reference.

A₁ amplifies the difference between these two currents and drives A₂, a free-running duty-cycle modulator, over several kilohertz of frequency to power the output transistor and the heater.

Generally, when power is applied to the circuit, A₁ attains a negative saturation, forcing A₂'s output to a positive one. The LM395 then turns on and the oven warms. When the oven is within 1°C of the desired setting, A₂ becomes unsaturated and runs at a duty cycle dependent upon A₁'s output voltage. The duty cycle is determined by the temperature difference between the oven and the setpoint. For the given values, the circuit will maintain an oven temperature at 75°C, ±0.1°C. □

Absolute-value amplifier uses just one op amp

by Larry Mitchell
Omnimedical, Paramount, Calif.

In many applications, certain functions within a circuit require the absolute value of the input voltage, and generally two or more operational amplifiers are needed to obtain this value. However, this design reduces the op-amp requirement to one. It inverts negative input voltages and leaves the polarity of positive input voltages unchanged.

Modulus. The circuit uses only one 741 operational amplifier to achieve absolute-value amplification. Accuracy within 15 millivolts for low values of input, $V_{in} < < 0.5$ V, is attained by using standard diodes and resistors in the circuit and having a gain of unity.

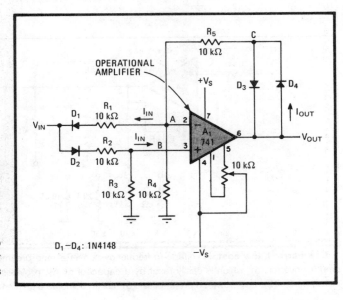

As shown in the figure, op amp A_1 serves as the unity-gain amplifier. When the input is negative, $V_{in} = -V$, diode D_1 conducts, thus producing voltage $V_c = -(-V + I_{in}R_D)$ at point c where R_D is the forward-bias resistance of the diode and I_{in} is the input current. Because the amplifier gain is unity, I_{in} is equal to the output current I_{out}. The output voltage is the sum of the voltages at point c and the drop across forward-biased diode D_4. Thus, $V_{out} = -(-V + I_{out}R_D) + I_{out}R_D = V$.

For positive inputs, $V_{in} = V$, D_2 conducts and produces voltage $(V - I_{in}R_D)/2$ at point b. Because the potential difference between points a and b is zero, the voltage at point a is also $(V - I_{in}R_D)/2$. Since D_1 is reverse-biased, there is no current through resistor R_1.

Therefore the voltage at point a is due to the two resistors, R_4 and R_5, acting as a divider. This condition produces a voltage $(V - I_{out}R_D)$ at point c. D_4 adds an additional voltage of $I_{out}R_D$ volts. The output is again $V_{out} = V$. Diode D_3 eliminates latchup by allowing the output to drive the inverting input negative when V_{in} approaches 0 V.

When the circuit has standard diodes and unity gain, equal conduction currents are produced through the diodes, resulting in an accuracy of within 15 millivolts. Voltage gains other than unity may be obtained by altering the resistor values. The amplification factors are R_5/R_1 for the inverting port and, for the noninverting port, $(R_4 + R_5)/(2 R_4)$ when $R_2 = R_3$. ☐

OTA multiplier converts to two-quadrant divider

by Henrique S. Malvar
Department of Electrical Engineering, University of Brazilia, Brazil

An inexpensive two-quadrant divider that is useful in tunable and tracking filters and special-purpose modulators and demodulators may be built using an operational transconductance amplifier (see figure). This circuit is based upon a multiplier circuit by W. G. Jung[1].

The desired circuit response is achieved by placing the CA3080 multiplier within the feedback loop of the 308 comparator. This method implements the divider function more easily than—and just as accurately as—the logarithmic and antilog converters often employed.

The transfer function of the circuit is given by:

$$V_{out}/V_{in} = -(1+k)/kR_2 g_m = -[2(1+k)V_T/kR_2 I_B]$$

where k = the resistance scaling ratio and $g_m = I_B/2V_T$ for the CA3080. V_T is the thermal voltage (26 millivolts at 23°C). The divider gain is thus inversely proportional to the input bias current, I_B. The plot in the figure shows the divider's nearly ideal response. Gain measurements were made with a selective voltmeter having a bandwidth of 10 hertz (HP 3581C) to eliminate noise effects—the circuit's linearity extends over five decades.

The offset of the 308 is also amplified as the circuit's bias current is reduced. Thus, I_B's lower limit should be around 20 nanoamperes. Also, the compensating capacitor must be at least equal to $A_{max} \times 30$ picofarads, where A_{max} is the maximum attenuation given by the divider circuit. The circuit uses a 300-pF capacitor because the maxiumum attenuation is 20 decibels.

The circuit's response to temperature variations is minimal, but in critical applications compensation is necessary for V_T. A temperature-compensating resistor having a thermal coefficient of 0.33% per °C for the resistor value kR_1 is used in this instance. ☐

References
1. W. G. Jung, "Get gain control of 80 to 100 dB," Electronic Design, June 21, 1974, pp. 94 – 99.

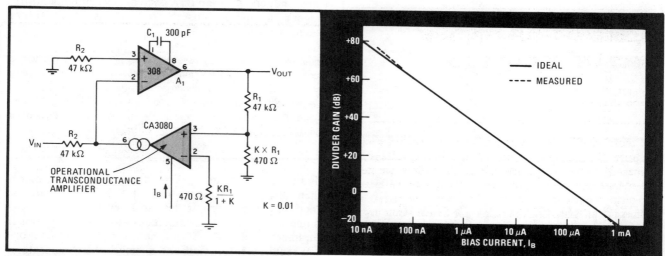

Inverse. A basic two-chip multiplier is easily transformed into a two-quadrant divider by the appropriate feedback. This scheme is simpler, no less accurate, and less costly than those using log and antilog converters. Circuit linearity extends to five decades of control current, I_B. Except for the most critical applications, temperature compensation is not required.

OTAs and op amp form voltage-controlled equalizer

by Henrique S. Malvar
University of Brazilia, Brazil

An audio equalizer usually employs a manual control to regulate frequencies. However, with just two operational transconductance amplifiers, an op amp, and a constant-current source, a simple voltage-controlled audio-equal-izer section can be made that, in effect, automatically controls the waveforms of a system. This section (a) can control a graphic equalizer of an audio system or, through a microprocessor, equalize the generated output from a speech or music synthesizer.

The transfer function of the circuit, H(s), is defined as $V_o(s)/V_{in}(s)$, or:

$$\frac{s^2C_1C_2 + s(C_2G_3 + C_1[G_4 + G_3 - (bg_{m1}/a)]) + G_3G_4}{s^2C_1C_2 + s(C_2G_3 + C_1[G_4 + G_3 - (bg_{m2}/a)]) + G_3G_4}$$

where $g_{m1} = I_{B1}/2V_t$ is the transconductance of OTA U_1, $g_{m2} = I_{B2}/2V_T$ is the transconductance of U_2, V_t is the volt equivalent of temperature (26 millivolts at 300 K) $G_3 = 1/R_3$, and $G_4 = 1/R_4$. Bias currents I_{B1} and I_{B2} alter only the first-order terms of H(s)—the requirement for a bump equalizer.

The gain at frequency ω_o, which is given by $1/(R_3R_4C_1C_2)^{1/2}$, is flat when the externally applied bias currents I_{B1} and I_{B2} are equal. A boost in equalizer gain is attained for $I_{B2} > I_{B1}$ and *vice versa*. As a result, a positive value for control voltage V_c leads to a boost response, and a negative value for V_c results in a loss.

The gain versus frequency response (b) measured by the circuit corresponds to control voltages +4 volts, +2 v, 0 v, −2 v, and −4 v. The curve shows that the equalizer provides gain for positive voltages and attenuation for negative values. With the given values, voltage dividers R_2 and bR_2 (b is a constant) keep the signal levels at the inputs of U_1 and U_2 within their permitted linear range. The 400-microampere constant-current source can be implemented with a pnp transistor or a p-channel field-effect transistor. In addition, because the transconductance of an OTA decreases with temperature, the current source must have a positive temperature coefficient of about 0.3%/°C. □

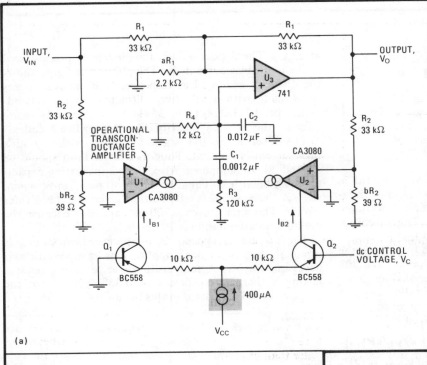

(a)

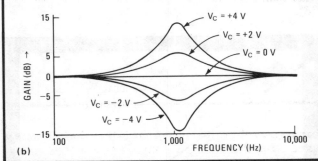

(b)

Equalizer. The circuit (a) uses two operational transconductance amplifiers CA3080, a 741 op amp, and a 400-microampere constant-current source to obtain a voltage-controlled audio-equalizer section. The parameters a and b are constants for voltage-dividing resistors R_1 and R_2. The measured frequency response (b) is attained for control voltages of +4 V, +2 V, 0 V, −2 V, and −4 V.

Diode plus op amp provide double-threshold function

by Pavel Novak
Fraunhofer Institute for Solid State Technology, Munich, West Germany

Medical instruments that produce a signal or alarm when physiological measurements like heart rate or blood pressure reach undesirable levels need window comparators, which usually comprise two operational amplifiers each (a). But a new circuit cuts the op-amp requirement by half and achieves the comparators' double-threshold function by means of a simple diode.

When input voltage V_{in} reverse-biases diode D_1, V_{in} appears at the op amp's noninverting input (b). In addi-

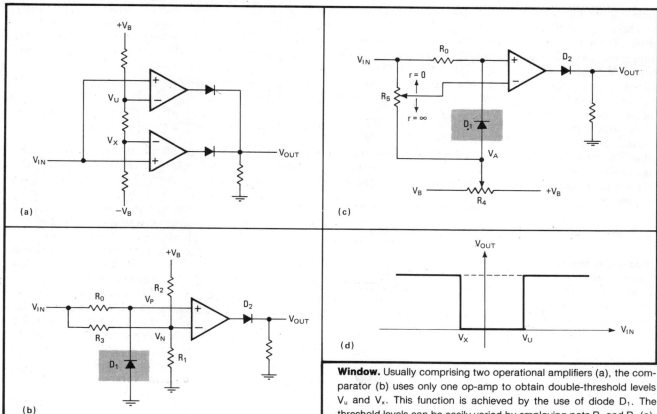

Window. Usually comprising two operational amplifiers (a), the comparator (b) uses only one op-amp to obtain double-threshold levels V_u and V_x. This function is achieved by the use of diode D_1. The threshold levels can be easily varied by employing pots R_4 and R_5 (c), and the window characteristic of the comparator is shown in (d).

tion, inverting input voltage V_n is the sum of supply voltage V_b and V_{in}. For this condition, $V_{in} = V_p$ (noninverting input voltage), and switching occurs when $V_p = V_n$. As a result, the upper threshold voltage V_u is now written as $V_u = V_b R_1/(R_1 + R_2)$.

On the other hand, when the input voltage forward biases D_1, the voltage at the noninverting input is $-V_d$, where V_d is the voltage across the diode under a forward-bias condition. The relationship for this second threshold voltage is now: $V_x = -V_b(R_3/R_2) - V_d$

$[1 + R_3(1/R_1 + 1/R_2)]$ when $V_u \geq 0$ and $V_x \leq -V_d$.

This particular circuit leaves no room for threshold-voltage adjustment, but may be modified through the use of two potentiometers (c). Potentiometer R_4 sets D_1's reference potential, V_a. In addition, resistors R_1 and R_2 are replaced with pot R_5. The new set of threshold voltages are given by: $V_u = V_a$ and $V_x = V_a - V_d(1+r)$, where $r = R_3/R_1$. The window $V_u - V_x$ is valid when it is greater than or equal to V_d. Its characteristics are shown in (d). □

Active potentiometer tunes common-mode rejection

by Jerald Graeme
Burr-Brown Research Corp., Tucson, Ariz.

A bipolar variable resistance may be simulated by a potentiometer in conjunction with an operational amplifier and four matched resistors. This active potentiometer controls the relative amounts of positive and negative op-amp feedback and eliminates the need for a buffer

when employed as a common-mode–rejection trimming circuit. Also, this adjustment circuit makes CMR tuning possible in either direction and is capable of providing output offsetting.

As an example, the circuit may be used with instrumentation amplifier INA101 to fine-tune its CMR. The values attained with this adjustment circuit range from 80 to 110 decibels for a gain of 1 and from 106 to 130 dB for a gain of 100, respectively.

Control over the resistance presented by the adjustment circuit across the terminals 1 and 2 is obtained by potentiometer R_v (see figure) that varies the relative amounts of positive and negative feedback around op amp U_2. The polarity of this resistance and its magnitude is given by $R_I = [(2x - 1)R_v]/(1 + xR_v/R)$.

The circuit's performance is limited by the op amp used. Any dc errors of the amplifier are reflected at the input terminal of the adjustment circuit as $V_{os} + I_{os}R$, where V_{os} and I_{os} are the input offset voltage and current. Similarly, noise introduced at this terminal is equal to $(e^2_{ni} + 2i^2_{ni}R^2)^{1/2}$, where e_{ni} and i_{ni} are the op amp input noise voltage and current, respectively.

As amplifier bandwidth can pose a problem if inadequate, the feedback must be set at levels that optimize this characteristic. If R is small compared with that being trimmed, the feedback factor is ½, giving a circuit bandwidth that is half the unity gain bandwidth of the op amp used. □

Bipolar potentiometer. Multiple-feedback op-amp circuit provides a variable resistance that is bipolar. This active bipolar potentiometer allows common-mode–rejection trimming in either direction for instrumentation amplifier INA101. With this adjustment circuit, common-mode rejection can be trimmed over a wide range.

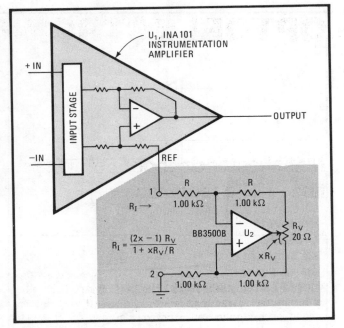

OPTOELECTRONICS

Manchester decoder optimizes fiber-optic receiver

by Dwayne Yount
Measurex Corp., Cupertino, Calif.

Using a low-cost high-speed optical receiver and a simple Manchester II decoder circuit, this inexpensive fiber-optic receiver accepts data at rates of 10 megabits per second and higher and from a distance of at least 1 kilometer. Because the Manchester code minimizes any frequency drift in the receiver, the circuit works well for such fiber optic communication systems and in addition facilitates the use of an automatic gain control.

The optical signal is detected by the p-i-n photodiode D_1 (see figure), and the corresponding electrical current is then amplified by the optical receiver U_1. This receiver output is also converted to TTL levels by U_1. The Manchester-coded data is next fed into the delay line, which provides a maximum delay of 100 nanoseconds. The MCODE signal is delayed by 50 ns, 80 ns, and 100 ns to provide additional three signals M_{50}, M_{80}, and M_{100}.

MCODE and M_{50} are fed into the exclusive-OR gate U_2, whose output is inverted by U_3 to produce the $DATA_1$ signal. Gate U_4 combines M_{80} and M_{100} to produce a clean 20-ns-wide (clock 1) pulse that is used to clock the D-type flip-flop U_5. The clock 2 output of U_5 clocks U_6 only when the data makes a transition. D-latch U_6 reproduces the original data at the $\overline{Q}_2$ output.

The AGC and the receiver gain of 60 decibels optimize the signal-to-noise ratio. As a result, the circuit is capable of handling optical powers of the level of 1 microwatt. The self-clocking ability of the Manchester code makes it possible to recover the clock from the data. □

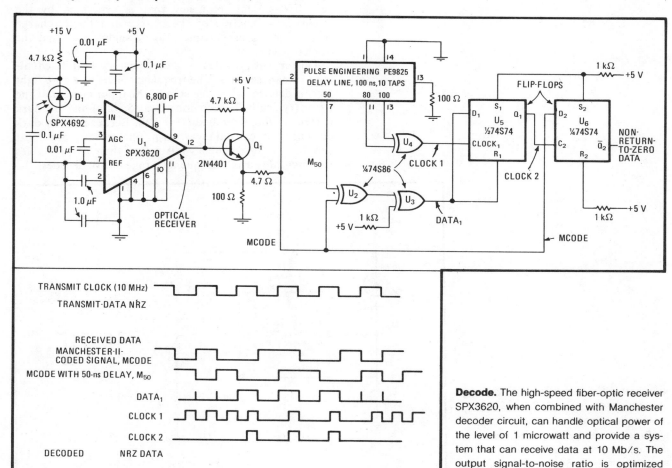

Decode. The high-speed fiber-optic receiver SPX3620, when combined with Manchester decoder circuit, can handle optical power of the level of 1 microwatt and provide a system that can receive data at 10 Mb/s. The output signal-to-noise ratio is optimized using AGC and a 60-dB receiver gain.

Photocurrent-to-frequency converter notes light levels

by Robert Nowotny, *Institute for the Study of Radium and Nuclear Physics, University of Vienna, Austria*

Illumination levels are usually measured in voltage for photometric and photographic applications. However, this circuit detects them in terms of hertz with a converter that uses the current-source characteristics of photodiodes, under reverse bias, to transform light levels into frequency.

The current, I_{ph}, obtained from the photodiode charges integrating capacitor C_1 to a voltage that is slightly greater than the threshold level of the ICM7555 timer (a). As a result of the charging, the timer turns on and C_1 discharges down to the lower trigger level. The timer is shut off once this level is hit, and a new charging and discharging cycle is started.

T_{ch} is the charging time and is given by $\Delta V \times C_1 / SE$, where ΔV is the voltage excursion between two threshold levels, E is the illuminance, and S is the diode response, which is a function of wavelength. At a wavelength of 800 nanometers, the response for p-i-n photodiode BPX66 is typically 0.5 microampere per microwatt irradiance. The sensitivity for an unfiltered tungsten light source (2,856 K) and a diode having an area of 1 millimeter square is 10 nA per lux illuminance.

Since ΔV is adjustable at pin 5 of the timer, the converter is calibrated with a voltage divider. C_1 is chosen through $C_1 = SE_{max}/\Delta V f_{max}$, where f_{max} is the maximum frequency that may be produced by the circuit. The actual frequency that is generated by the circuit is a function of the charge and the discharge times. The discharge time (T_d) depends on C_1 and the discharge current.

This circuit provides 10 pulses per lux with T_d equaling 450 nanoseconds. The frequency offset at a zero light level is determned by the sum of the input current of the timer (typically 20 picoamperes at 5 volts) and the dark current of the photodiode (≈ 1 nA). Because of low dark current and capacitance, p-i-n photodiodes are most suitable. A low-frequency offset (less than 1 Hz) enables the circuit to cover a frequency range of five decades. □

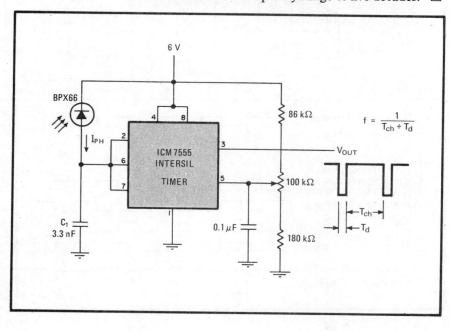

Illumination level. Photodiode BPX66 and timer ICM7555 in the astable mode directly convert photocurrent to frequency. Capacitor C_1 is charged by the photocurrent and discharged by the internal switch of the timer. A voltage divider at pin 5 calibrates the converter to measure illumination levels.

Opto-isolated RS-232 interface achieves high data rate

by Vojin G. Oklobdzija
Xerox-Microelectronics, El Segundo, Calif.

When signals originating from isolated sources are transferred to a destination at a different voltage, coupling circuitry must be used to minimize signal distortion and interference. Unfortunately this circuitry slows down data-transmission rates. However, General Instrument's dual-phototransistor opto-isolator MCT66 may be used to isolate an RS-232 interface and still achieve a relatively high data rate of 9,600 bits per second.

The opto-isolated RS-232 interface (a) uses the MCT66, two diodes, an inverter, and a resistor. If pull-up resistors were used instead of transistors Q_1 and Q_3, the rising edge of the signal would be slow and thus would limit the transmission rate to below 1,200 b/s.

This limiting depends on the values of the resistors and the length of the RS-232 cable. However, if the pull-up resistor's value is reduced below 1 kilohm, intolerable power dissipation occurs.

This circuit not only achieves high data rates but also enables the polarity of the signal to be changed, without using an additional inverter, by altering the connections between transistors Q_1 and Q_2 or Q_3 and Q_4 (b). □

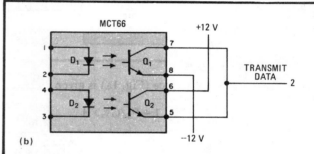

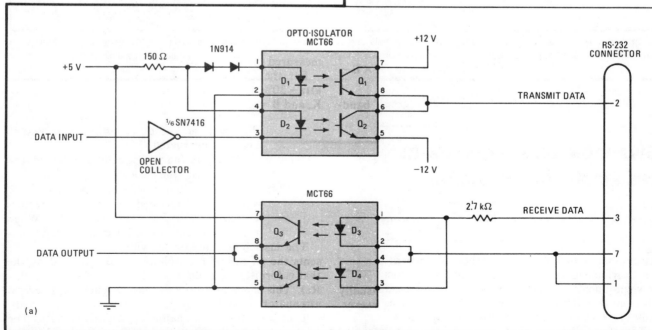

Isolation. General Instrument's dual-phototransistor opto-isolator MCT66 isolates the RS-232 interface (a) and achieves a high data rate of 9,600 b/s. The signal's polarity may be changed by altering the connections between Q_1 and Q_2 or Q_3 and Q_4 (b).

Optical coupler isolates comparator inputs

by Dennis J. Eichenberg
Cleveland, Ohio

Many dc-comparator applications need complete signal isolation. However, Motorola's optically isolated linear coupler MOC5010 eases this problem by eliminating the complex circuitry that is required with other techniques. The circuit's use of a single-ended power supply further simplifies the design.

The comparator circuit (see figure) compares two 0-to-12-volt signals that must be completely isolated. Resistor R_1, calculated for a current of 40 milliamperes, creates an acceptable current from V_{in} for the light-emitting diode of optocoupler A_1. Because there is an offset voltage at the output of A_1 ($V_{in} = 0$ v), the voltage at the inverting input of A_2 is made equal to the voltage at the noninverting input by adjusting the offset trimmer potentiomenter R_4. This adjustment is done when V_{in} and V_{ref} are zero. Resistors R_5 and R_6 protect A_2 by limiting surge current.

Potentiometers R_2 and R_3 permit the slope of the input voltage for A_2 to be adjusted at the maximum V_{in} and V_{ref} by a desired ratio. When V_{in} exceeds V_{ref} by this ratio, the output goes high. Hysteresis may be provided by connecting an appropriate resistor from the output to the comparator's noninverting input. □

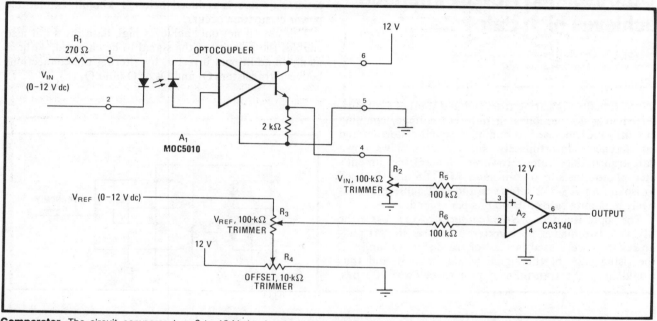

Comparator. The circuit compares two 0-to-12-V dc signals and provides complete isolation between the two signals. The circuit uses optocoupler MOC5010 to provide isolation and requires a single-ended power supply. Potentiometer R_4 balances the offset voltage.

Swapable fiber-optic parts ease isolation problems

by Jim Herman
Motorola Semiconductor Sector, Phoenix, Ariz.

Assembling opto-isolators from their component parts to meet various high-voltage, high-frequency applications is now simplified with the introduction of interchangeable fiber-optic emitters and detectors. These devices can be built at a lower cost than conventional hybrids.

Therefore, systems such as a simple and effective 25-megahertz analog transmission channel and a 20-megabit-a-second emitter-coupled-logic data-handling system, which provide ac and dc isolation up to 50,000 volts, may be easily constructed.

A light-emitting diode and an optically-coupled photosensitive detector make up the basic optical isolator (Fig. la, p. 124). The plastic cable-splice bushing and plastic retainer caps housing the ferruled emitters and detectors are manufactured by AMP Inc., Harrisburg, Pa. When assembled, the components form an isolator that measures 0.75 inch long and 0.5 in. wide.

Characteristics of the isolator are determined by the selected emitter and detector. In particular, the interchangeable detectors provide the designer with several options that include interfacing with TTL or ECL loads, wide bandwidths, and analog or digital formats. The isolation voltage of the device is directly related to the separation between the LED and the detector, the package material, its size and shape, and the value of the

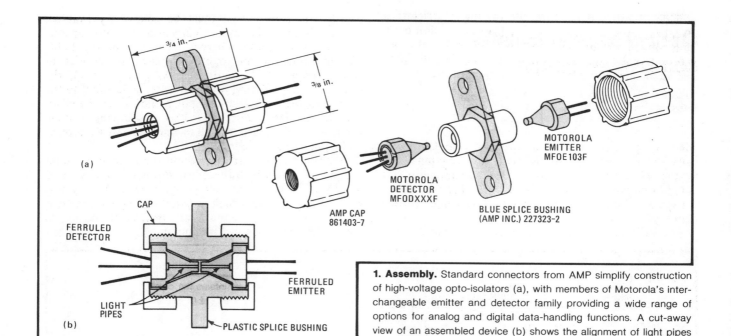

1. Assembly. Standard connectors from AMP simplify construction of high-voltage opto-isolators (a), with members of Motorola's interchangeable emitter and detector family providing a wide range of options for analog and digital data-handling functions. A cut-away view of an assembled device (b) shows the alignment of light pipes that contribute to isolator's high efficiency and excellent isolation.

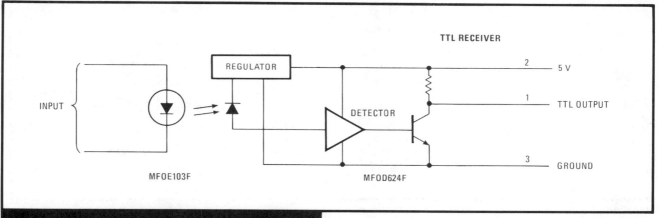

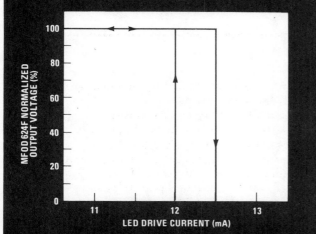

2. Applications. An isolator that can handle 500-kb/s data rates for TTL loads is configured with the MFOE103F emitter and MFOD 624F detector. The device's transfer function is also very sharp. Replacing the receiver with a 404F detector converts the unit to one that delivers a 10-Mb/s data rate. When the MFOC600 receiver is added, an isolator will provide 20-Mb/s data rates to ECL loads.

parasitic capacity (C_C). This capacity determines the amount of ac protection.

The actual isolation (breakdown) voltage may easily be determined by measuring the voltage potential across the isolator from input to output at a prespecified leakage current such as 80 microamperes.

The coupler (lb) contains light pipes that provide efficient coupling while maintaining a large separation between the emitter and detector. As a result, the input and output have excellent ac and dc isolation. A wide selection of emitters and detectors are available.

Among the devices that may be readily assembled is a 25-MHz analog isolator built with the MFOE103F emitter and the MFOD104F pin detector. The transfer function of this device will be linear, providing a 0-to-20-μA pin-diode output for a 0-to-75-milliampere LED driving current.

Similarly, a 500-kilobit TTL isolator, Fig. 2, is easily built with the MFOE103F emitter and the MFOD624F integrated receiver. For wider bandwidths, the MFOD 404F integrated detector preamplifier and the MFOC 600 receiver circuit may be used. This combination will provide 10-Mb/s data rates for driving TTL loads or 20-Mb/s rates for driving ECL loads. In addition to high-voltage optical isolation, this isolator will also provide automatic gain control to stabilize output signals and an analog output port for status monitoring. □

OSCILLATORS

High-frequency sweep oscillator uses discrete components

by Charles A. Walton
Walton Electronics, Los Gatos, Calif.

Offering a wide frequency range and low distortion, this high-frequency sweep oscillator uses discrete components to deliver a clean sine wave of 0.3 to 70 megahertz with a control voltage of 0.5 to 2.5 volts. The oscillator's total harmonic distortion factor is less than 3%.

The circuit (a) uses a triple-stage inverter. It has an overall positive feedback at a frequency where each stage has a phase lag of 60° in addition to an inversion lag of 180°, resulting in a total phase lag of 720°. The oscillator frequency is varied by controlling the collector's s pply voltage and current—a higher collector supply voltage results in a higher frequency of oscillation.

By using complementary npn and pnp transistors, symmetrical rise and fall times are generated for each stage, thereby eliminating even harmonics. In addition, diode clamps in each stage prevent saturation and minimize odd harmonics. The third harmonic generated is 360° out of phase in successive stages (b).

The oscillator output is taken from a pair of successive stages and subtracted with a differential amplifier, thus canceling the third harmonic. The fifth harmonic is damped by the bandwidth limitation of each stage. Moderate decoupling between stages using 100-ohm resistors

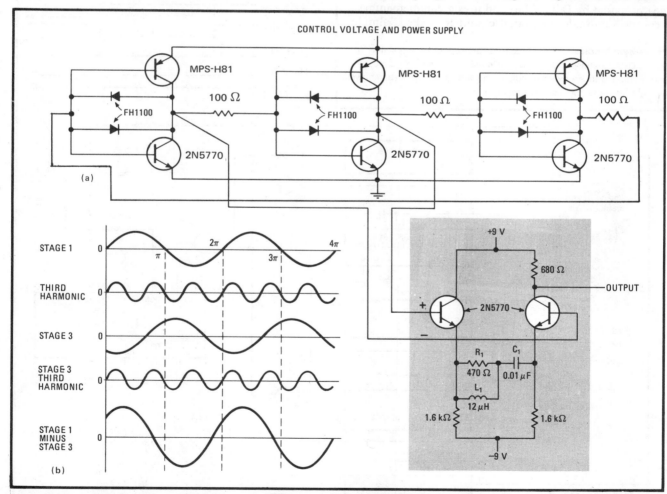

Sweeping oscillator. Increasing the supply voltage of this oscillator (a) reduces the stage-time delay, thus increasing the frequency of oscillation. Also, harmonic distortion is low due to the use of complementary npn and pnp transistors and the diodes. R_1, L_1, and C_1 shape the high-frequency envelope. The differential-amplifier output cancels third harmonic (b). Signal amplitude is 0.8 V peak to peak at 15 MHz.

avoids parasitic oscillation. As a result, the overall low harmonic distortion allows a good-quality sine wave to be created.

The signal amplitude is 0.5 v peak to peak at 3 MHz, 0.7 v at 10 MHz, and 0.8 v at 15 MHz. The differential-amplifier stage is a convenient point to shape the amplitude versus frequency characteristic.

The high-frequency sweep oscillator, used in a proximity electronic access system for control and identification, drives a sensing coil and searches through the high-frequency spectrum (3 to 30 MHz) for resonances in a credit-card key. The resonances, once they are found, are used to determine the identity of the bearer. □

C-MOS IC achieves triggered phase-locked oscillations

by N. Miron, M. N. Ion, and D. Sporea
Central Institute of Physics, Romania

The application of dual vernier interpolation to time-interval measurements requires a triggered phase-locked oscillator that is phase-synchronized with the external trigger signal. This circuit (a) is a modification of the idea proposed by D. C. Chu[1] and uses a complementary-MOS medium-scale integrated circuit to make it simple

and inexpensive.

Prior to the arrival of an external-phase–synchronization pulse, the oscillation frequency (f_1) of the voltage-controlled oscillator is in phase with the reference frequency (f_o). In the quiescent lock state, the positive transitions of the mixer and counter output occur at the

Phase-synchronized. This triggered phase-locked oscillator (a) uses a C-MOS phase-locked–loop CD4046 and achieves phase synchronization with an external pulse. The timing diagram (b) shows typical waveforms for different sections of the oscillator.

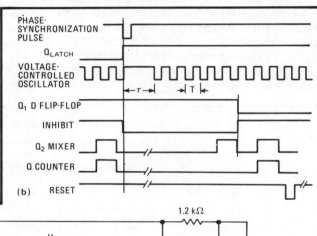

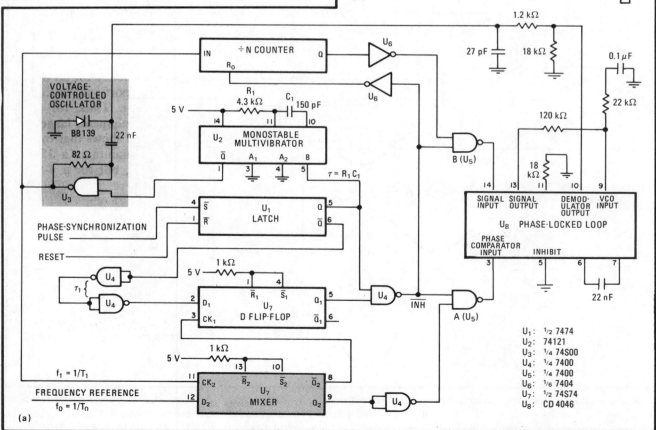

same time, thereby satisfying $f_o - f_1 = f_1/N$ or in terms of period, $T_1 = (1 + 1/N)T_o$.

The arrival of the phase-synchronization pulse sets the latch whose output through the one-shot multivibrator U_2 inhibits the VCO (b) for a time that is determined by R_1C_1 ($\tau = 600$ ns). However, when the VCO starts again with a zero phase shift, the signal $\overline{INH}$ (inhibit) resets the divide-by-N counter.

This $\overline{INH}$ signal through NAND gates A and B also inhibits the three-state phase comparator (U_8) that will remain in a high-impedance state between the arrival of the phase-synchronization pulse and the first negative transition of mixer output $\overline{Q}_2$. The $\overline{INH}$ state is changed by this sequence, thereby enabling gates A and B and directing the mixer and counter outputs to the phase-comparator inputs.

The delay τ_1 introduced at the latch's output $\overline{Q}$ avoids locking a possible initial mixer negative transition that is not related to phase crossover. The circuit is set to the initial state with an external RESET signal. ☐

References
1. D. C. Chu, "The triggered phase-locked oscillator," Hewlett-Packard Journal, Vol. 29, Aug. 1978, p. 8.

POWER SUPPLIES

Parallel power MOS FETs increase circuit current capacity

by Herb Saladin and Al Pshaenich
Motorola Semiconductor Products Sector, Phoenix, Ariz.

A fast high-voltage and -current pulse is often needed to evaluate the characteristics of a switching power device. For such applications, the semiconductor switch must be much faster than the device under test. Power MOS field-effect transistors serve this function well, but are limited by their current-carrying capability. However, this current capability can be increased without altering the switching speed of the generated pulse by paralleling the transistors.

Power MOS FETs Q_1 through Q_{15} (Fig. 1) are connect-

ed in parallel to obtain 150 amperes of peak pulsed current for the system. Initially, the FET with the highest transconductance (g_{fs}) draws the largest drain current and consequently causes high dissipation. The resulting temperature rise increases the drain-source on-resistance $r_{ds(on)}$ and self-limits the drain current. This process will continue until all of the FETs in the circuit have equal drain currents.

Two p-channel FETs (Q_{16} and Q_{17}) are connected in parallel to provide the drive current for the MOS FET switch. These FETs are turned on by the negative-going input pulse. Limiting resistor R_2 and speed-up capacitor C_2 in the drain path of Q_{16} and Q_{17} feed the 15 gate circuits of Q_1 through Q_{15}. For simplicity, only the gate circuits of Q_1 and Q_{15} are shown, each formed by a directly coupled resistor, a speed-up capacitor, and back-to-back zener diodes for protection.

In the circuit, approximately 150 A at 140 volts is switched extremely fast, with voltage turn-on time being

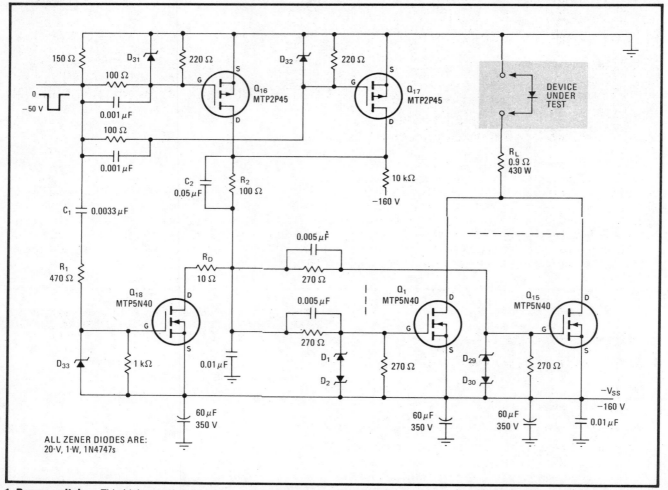

1. Power switcher. This high-speed and high-current semiconductor switch uses 15 n-channel power MOS FETs in parallel to achieve the circuit capability of 150 A of peak pulsed current. Unmatched FETs are used because the self-limiting ability of each FET tends to equalize the drain current. A low–duty-cycle, 50-V input drive pulse has a rise time of 10 ns.

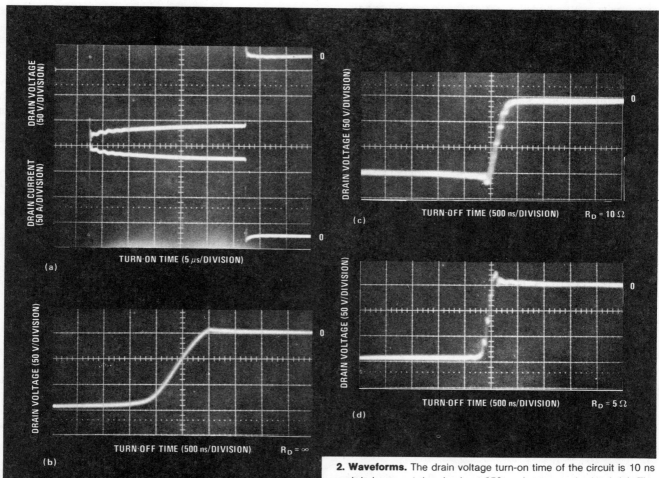

2. Waveforms. The drain voltage turn-on time of the circuit is 10 ns and drain current rises in about 250 ns due to reactive load. (a). The drain voltage turns off in about 1 μs (b) without clamp Q_{18}. With the clamp the turn-off time is reduced to 0.2 μs (c). The FET switch turns off faster as the value of resistance R_d is reduced (d).

less than 10 nanoseconds and current rise time about 250 ns (Fig. 2a). The turn-off time for the power switch is improved with the n-channel FET clamp Q_{18}, which turns on at the input pulse's trailing edge and supplies a reverse gate voltage to the power switch. The drain voltage turn-off time of about 1 microsecond (Fig. 2b) is reduced to 0.2 μs with this clamp (Fig. 2c). Reducing resistor R_d further lessens turn-off time (Fig. 2d).

Extreme care must be exercised in the layout of the 15 parallel MOS FETs. Lead lengths must be kept as short as possible and rf bypass capacitors placed at several points along the source bus line to minimize reactive effects. A duty cycle of less than 1% is used to ensure safe operation. □

5-V converter powers EE-PROMs, RS-232-C drivers

by Richard A. McGrath
Studio 7 Technical Documentation, San Carlos, Calif.

Many of today's electrically erasable programmable and electrically alterable read-only memories require different voltages from the RS-232-C drivers needed to interface them with microprocessors. This dc-to-dc converter changes 5 volts into ±11 v for these drivers and 21 v for programming or reading EE-PROMs. Because the RS-

TYPICAL TEST RESULTS FOR A 5-V SUPPLY				
Test point voltage (V)	Logic state of IH5143 analog switch, pin 15			
	Switch S_2 open		Switch S_2 closed (grounded)	
	Low	High	Low	High
MC1488* pin 1	−0.2	−11.8	−4.3	−13.5
MC1488* pin 14	+21.7	+10.6	+8.7	+7.5
2817 pin 1 1.5-kΩ load	+20.7	+10.7	+3.5	+3.0
+V_{output}	+22.4	+11.3	+9.4	+8.2
−V_{output}	−0.9	−12.4	−4.9	−14.0
*300-Ω load on output pin 3, logic high on pin 2				

232-C drivers and EE-PROMs operate at different time intervals and the circuit's switching time is much shorter than that of serial communication, power requirement conflicts do not occur.

Semiconductor Circuits' power converter U_1 can generate ±12 V or +24 V with the addition of single-pole double-throw switch S_1, diode D_1, and capacitor C_1(a). If S_1 is in position 1, ±12 V are produced. In position 2, this switch gives +24 V. In addition, D_1 ensures that a positive voltage is generated from pin 3 during switching, and surge voltages are suppressed by C_1.

The dc-to-dc converter (b) uses Intersil's analog switch S_1 (IH5143) to switch the converter more quickly from ±11 to +21 V. The switching is controlled by logic, and many voltages can be selected from the circuit with switch S_2 and the logic at pin 15 of S_1 (see table).

Any negative voltage across the drain-to-body junc-tion of the body-puller field-effect transistor of S_1 is stopped by diode D_2. Zener diode D_5 and resistor R_2 reduce +24 to +21 V when EE-PROM U_2 is programmed or read. In addition, this combination reduces ±12 to ±11 v, which powers RS-232-C driver U_3. Capacitor C_2 prevents voltage override when the switching frequency is about 5 kilohertz. Grounding resistor R_1 together with S_2 provides correct power switching for EE-PROMs when the circuit is turned on or off. The 5-V supply also is directly tapped in order to power one of the inputs of the EE-PROM.

Tradeoffs in memory organization (2-K by 8 bits), programming convenience, product availability, and power requirements led to the choice of Intel's 2817 EE-PROM for U_2. Many other voltages can be selected from this circuit, and as a result, any EE-PROM may be used in it. This cost-effective design eliminates bulky transformers and voltage regulators and thus requires only a few external components. It finds applications in lightweight airborne or robotic systems. □

Converter. The dc-to-dc converter (a) uses minimum components to generate ± 12 or +24 volts. To provide faster switching, mechanical switch S_1 is replaced with the Intersil's analog switch IH5143 (b). The switching of this converter is controlled by logic and used to program or read 2817 EE-PROMs or to power RS-232-C drivers.

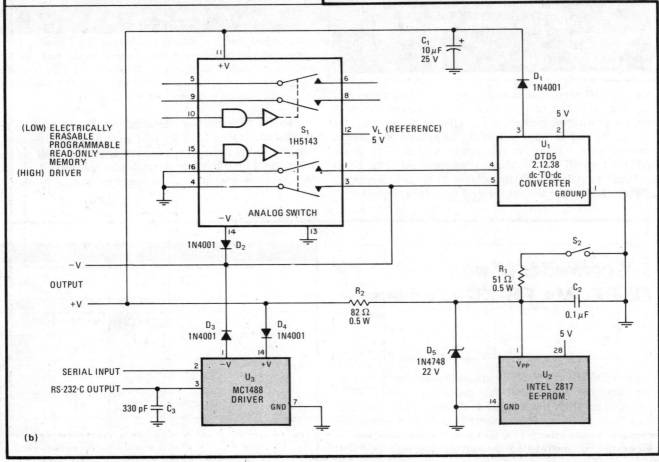

High frequencies, winding setup improve voltage conversion

by David W. Conway
Universal Engineering Corp., Cedar Rapids, Iowa

Designed to meet high-voltage requirements, this efficient and inexpensive dc-to-dc converter finds use in devices like photoflash equipment and capacitive-discharge ignition systems. The design produces 450 volts at 250 milliamperes from a 12-to-16-V dc supply. The high-power output and high efficiency of the circuit is attributed to high-frequency operation and the use of insulating tape between the layers of the transformer's secondary winding.

A push-pull–amplifier configuration comprising power field-effect transistors Q_3 and Q_4 is driven by integrated circuits U_1 through U_3. Oscillator U_1 generates 150 kilohertz, which is halved to 75 kHz by flip-flop U_2. The high-voltage output is adjusted with potentiometer R_1. When R_1 is at its minimum resistance, the output voltage is at its highest.

This converter is much smaller than competing designs because high frequencies are used. The output transformer's secondary is first wound on the bobbin. In addition, 400 turns of the secondary winding are composed of eight layers of about 50 turns a layer, with each layer insulated from the other. 3M's Permacel 0.0025-inch–thick insulating tape separates the layers.

The two layers of wire that make up the primary winding are referred to as sections A and B. A 48-in. piece of AWG No. 18 wire is folded in half to obtain a bifilar strand, 24 in. long, that is wound as section A on the bobbin. Six bifilar turns fill the cross section of the bobbin to form this layer. Similarly, section B is wound with six bifilar turns of AWG No. 18 wire on top of Section A. The windings are interconnected in series and properly phased to form a 24-turn primary winding. Scaling the turns ratio can provide additional output voltages as necessary. □

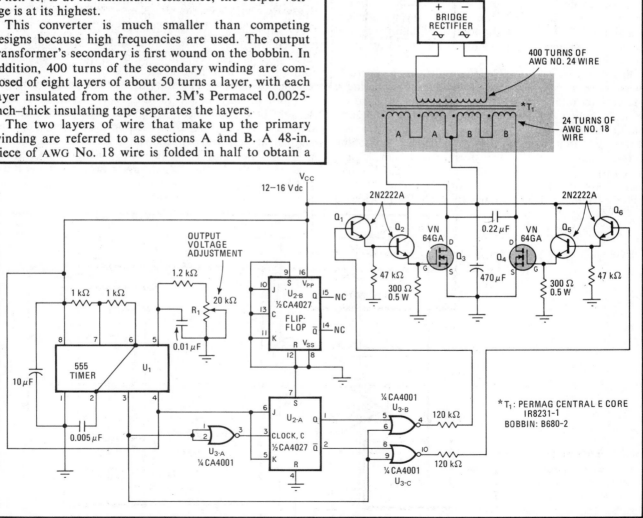

High-voltage converter. Oscillator U_1, frequency divider U_2, and buffer U_3 drive power FETs Q_3 and Q_4 in a push-pull configuration to generate 450 V at 250 mA. A power efficiency of about 90% is attributed to transformer's winding techniques and the use of high frequencies.

Generating a negative voltage for portable instruments

by J. D. McK. Watson, *Biomedical Engineering Research Group, University of Sussex, Falmer, Brighton, UK*

Many recently designed microcomputer-based portable instruments require +5- and −10-volt dc supplies. Though +5 v can be readily derived from a battery supply by means of a linear regulator, the latter needs a special circuit. This flyback converter presents a novel power supply design that uses just one operational amplifier and a few discrete components. The circuit efficiency is about 75% for a load of about 10 milliamperes, and the output voltage can be changed by substituting an alternative zener diode.

Operational amplifier U_1 functions as a current-sensing threshold switch and is capable of providing a wide output-voltage swing. This threshold is adjusted for optimum supply efficiency and output-voltage regulation. Q_1 is driven by the output of U_1 and operates as a saturating switch, with pulse transformer T_1 functioning as its collector load. The transformer is designed for a turns ratio of 1:1 with primary and secondary inductance of 3 millihenrys and a resistance of 1 ohm.

The current in T_1's primary through Q_1 provides a signal to the inverting input of U_1 whose noninverting input is fed from three sources. A portion of the op amp's output provides positive feedback to ensure fast switching, an ac signal from T_1's secondary results in the collapse of the flux before recycling, and a dc component tapped from the output lowers the threshold when the output exceeds zener diode D_2's breakdown voltage.

When the circuit is switched on, U_1 delivers a high output to Q_1 and turns it on. Current in the primary of T_1 increases linearly, developing a positive voltage at its secondary. This rising primary current also creates a voltage at the inverting input of U_1 that is sufficient to turn it off. As a result, the flux in T_1 collapses and the secondary current charges capacitor C_1. During this energy transfer, R_4 holds the noninverting input negative and inhibits the switch from turning on.

As subsequent cycles add charge to C_1, a point is reached when D_2 conducts and inhibits U_1 through R_5. This stage is disabled until the dc output voltage falls below the zener threshold, whereupon the circuit resumes oscillation. The amplitude of the output voltage is approximately equal to the zener voltage of D_2. Because of the nonlinear method of regulation, a small amount of ripple is superimposed on the output. For the component values shown, the ripple is of the order of 40 millivolts, but can be reduced by using a RC filter network at the output. Maximum power output is limited by the supply voltage and by the saturation current of T_1. □

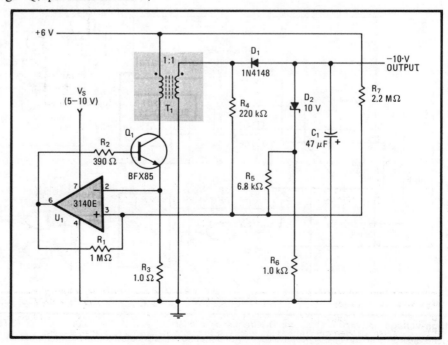

Flyback converter. This novel flyback converter uses just one op amp, U_1, pulse transformer T_1, and a few discrete components to provide a −10-V dc voltage. The supply ripple contents are low and the circuit efficiency is approximately 75%. Zener diode D_2 is used to set the output voltage.

External pass FET boosts regulated output voltage

by H. F. Nissink
Australian Maritime College, Tasmania, Australia

With a floating regulator and a power field-effect transistor acting as the external pass transistor, this power supply can deliver limited current and regulated high voltages. The supply's output voltage and current are adjustable, and the low drive requirement of the FET eliminates the need for Darlington-type stages. Regulators with low drop-out voltages can be designed easily because the power FET has a low on-resistance.

Floating regulator U_1's internal constant-current source of 1 milliampere develops a maximum voltage of 300 volts, serving as the regulator's reference voltage, across resistance chain R. The output voltage is compared with this, and an error voltage is applied to the gate of the power FET Q_1 to keep the load's current and voltage constant. Current-sense resistor R_s determines the maximum constant-current output, while potentiometer R_1 is used to adjust the output current between zero and the maximum value.

The regulated output voltage is adjustable in steps of 10 V from 200 to 300 V, and the maximum constant current is 50 mA. Switch S_1 selects the desired output voltage. Zener diode D_1 connected across the gate-source junctions of Q_1 provides extra gate protection. For a continuous output voltage control, a 100-kilohm potentiometer may replace R. □

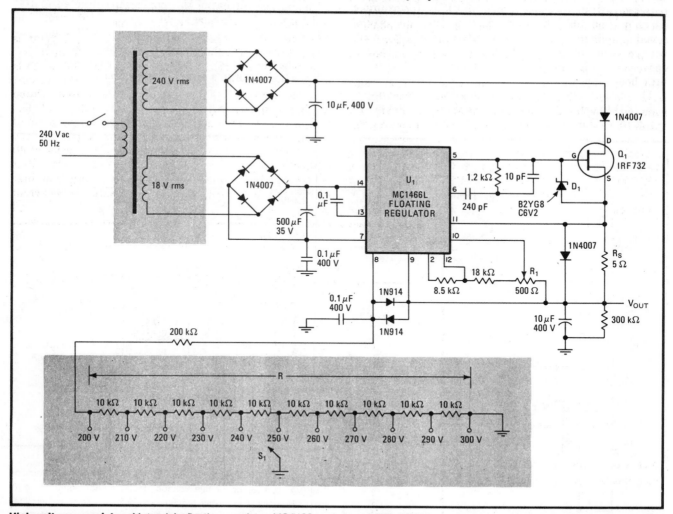

High-voltage regulator. Motorola's floating regulator MC1466 and power FET IRF732, serving as an external pass transistor, provide current-limited high voltage that is adjustable in steps of 10 V from 200 to 300 V. The maximum constant output current is 50 mA, and the FET's low drive requirement enables the regulator to boost the output regulated voltage.

Capacitive voltage doubler
forms ± 12-to- ± 15-V converter

by Tom Durgavich
National Semiconductor Corp., Santa Clara, Calif.

Pairing a capacitive voltage doubler with a regulator provides a simple solution to the problem of converting ± 12 volts dc into ± 15 v dc. Such a conversion is often required in systems using Intel's Multibus, for example, which puts out only ± 12 v dc. Such a conversion is often tional amplifiers and data converters to a guaranteed voltage swing of ± 10 v. Unlike conventional dc-to-dc converters, this approach is inexpensive and occupies little board space.

The circuit (a) uses a 5-watt audio power amplifier (LM384) to drive capacitive voltage doublers that generate ± 18 v. One doubler, consisting of capacitors C_1 and C_3 and diodes D_1 and D_3, generates +18 v and the other, consisting of C_2 and C_4 and D_2 and D_4, −18 v. The saturation voltage of the 384 op amp along with the voltage drop across the diodes prevents these voltages from ever reaching ± 24 v.

The power-amplifier clock input derived from the system clock keeps the switching waveform synchronous and random noise to a minimum. The clock input voltage and frequency can vary from 2 to 12 v peak to peak and 3 to 20 kilohertz, respectively. The 7-kHz square-wave oscillator (b) is used when the system clock is not available or synchronous operation is not desired.

The output current of this converter is limited to 100 milliamperes but can be slightly increased by providing the op amp with a good heat sink. The ± 18 v unregulated voltages may be increased to greater then ± 30 v by connecting diodes D_1 and D_2 to + 12-v and − 12-v sources instead of to a ground connection. □

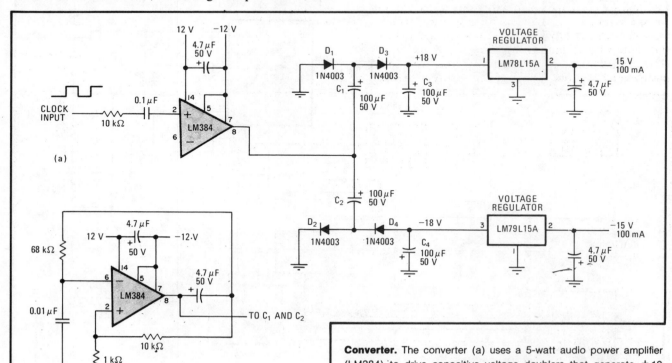

Converter. The converter (a) uses a 5-watt audio power amplifier (LM384) to drive capacitive voltage doublers that generate ± 18 volts. This voltage is further regulated to ± 15 V with three terminal regulators LM78L15A and LM79L15A. The square-wave oscillator (b) is used when synchronous operation is not desired or the system clock is not available. The cost is under $5.

Programmable source sets voltage of E-PROMs

by Ralph Tenny
George Goode & Associates, Dallas, Texas

Many erasable programmable read-only memories require varying voltages for different functions at pin 20. Intel's 2732 E-PROM, for example, multiplexes two functions on pin 20—the output enable and programming voltage input. It is desirable to have these inputs generated by a programmable source since the use of a relay to switch voltages is cumbersome, slowing down the circuit and adding a mechanical element to it. This programmable supply, controlled with two logic signals, provides an automatic selection of four voltages and has 0 volt as an off position.

This logic-controlled programmable voltage source (see figure) is composed of three integrated circuits, a voltage reference, and a few discrete components and has a slew rate of around 1 v per microsecond. However, this slew rate is limited by the operational amplifier (U_4). In addition, a constant slew rate for both the positive and negative swings of the supply is maintained by transistor Q_2, which pulls the output voltage down rapidly.

The binary-coded–decimal-to-decimal decoder in the circuit takes two logic input signals and converts them into four output signals. These outputs enable the four sections of switch U_3 that gate the operational amplifier's (U_4) input. The op amp along with transistors Q_1 and Q_2 forms a voltage regulator whose output is 11 times the input reference voltage. This 2.5-V reference is provided by U_1 and is tapped by potentiometers R_1, R_2, and R_3, which in turn produce the reference voltages needed to generate the desired programming voltages.

All the voltages needed for pin 20 are produced by means of this supply (as shown in the truth table). As a result, all 5-V E-PROMs, including the I2732A and I2764, may be programmed with this circuit. The supply is driven by the B port pins of the peripheral interface adapter MC6821.

The PIA lines that drive inputs A_1 and A_2 are terminated with pull-up resistors. This configuration produces a reset input of 11 (to U_2) that forces the programming voltage to 0 V. The performance of this circuit is adequate for all E-PROMs except for Motorola's MC68766. which requires a fast 12-V/μs slew rate. □

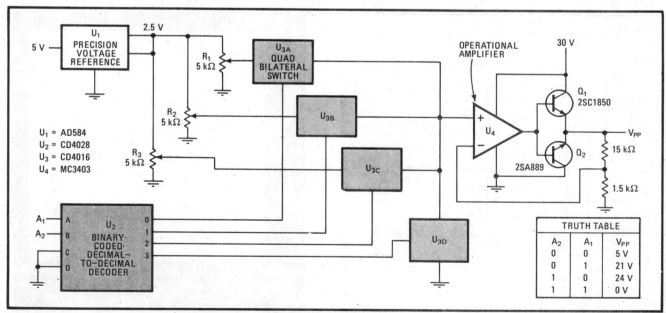

Programmable supply. Three ICs, a voltage reference and a few discrete components form this logic-controlled programmable voltage source with its approximately 1-V/μs slew rate. The supply is capable of providing four output voltages with 0 V as an off position.

External transistor boosts
load current of voltage regulator

by Dan Watson
Intersil Inc., Cupertino, Calif.

The current capability of Intersil's new low-power programmable voltage regulator may be increased from 40 milliamperes to 1 ampere through the use of an external npn pass transistor (a). The device is connected in parallel with the ICL7663's internal transistor.

The total current supplied by the regulator (I_r) is equal to the base current of the external pass transistor plus the load current of the internal pass transistor. The latter's emitter is situated at pin 2. A 100-ohm resistor is placed between the emitters of the two transistors, so that most of the load current will flow through the external device.

In addition, the circuit does not alter the programming ability of the regulator whose output (V_{output}) equals $(R_2/R_1)V_{set}$, where $V_{set} = 1.3$ volts. The device can regulate any voltage from 1.3 to 15.5 V for a load current up to 1 A. The load-current versus regulator-current characteristic (b) shows that for a 1.0-A load current, the regulator supplies only 16 mA, which is well within its operating range. A logic 0 or 1 at pin 5 turns the circuit on or off. ☐

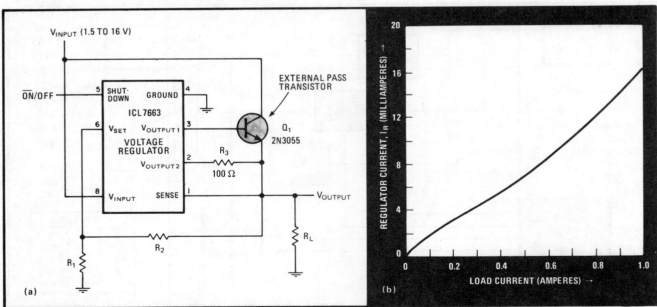

Booster. The circuit (a) uses an external npn pass transistor to boost the current capability of the voltage regulator ICL 7663. This transistor carries the bulk of the load current. The graph (b) shows that for a load current of 1 ampere, the regulator supplies only 16 mA.

Voltage translator switches auxiliary voltages when needed

by Ralph Tenny
George Goode & Associates Inc., Dallas, Texas

Low-drain auxiliary voltages, which are needed for short periods of time in many devices, can be supplied by dc-to-dc converters provided they are used continuously. If not, their presence constitutes an unnecessary and excessive power drain. However, this circuit allows these voltages to be switched on only when they are needed, thereby reducing power consumption and optimizing conversion efficiencies. In addition, the circuit's input drive is programmable, and the translator's operation may be controlled remotely.

Only the converter stage that is preceded by voltage translator Q_1 is shown (see figure) because the circuit's input can be driven from many sources—the bit-per-second rate generator of a microcomputer board, a peripheral-interface adapter port, TTL, and the output of a free-running timer, to mention only a few.

However, the main power input to the converter is a separate voltage supply. For example, it could be that only a 5-volt bus is available, and then the doubler shown may have to be replaced with tripler or quadrupler circuitry. Assuming a 9-v source is available, +15v is possible using this circuit; +18v would require a tripler.

This circuit produces approximately +8 v and −8 v at 30 milliamperes each when powered with 5 v. The conversion efficiency is about 75% and depends upon the saturation voltages of transistors Q_2 and Q_3 and the voltage drop across the diode, as does the output voltage. To reduce the voltage drop across the rectifier, the silicon diodes should be replaced with Schottky rectifiers. This change improves both conversion efficiency and output voltage by about 8%. □

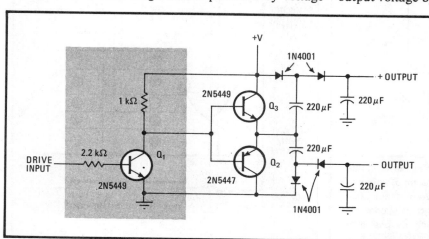

Part-time. When voltage translator Q_1 precedes the dc converter stage, the drive input can be generated by the logic signals regardless of the converter input voltage. The circuit allows the auxiliary voltages to be switched on when needed. Also, the circuit's operation can be controlled remotely.

SIGNAL DETECTORS & DISCRIMINATORS

Frequency comparator uses synchronous detection

by Israel Yuval
Video Logic Corp., Sunnyvale, Calif.

There are many different ways to monitor a frequency but most have the disadvantage that they also detect any noise inherent in the circuit along with the desired waveform. This circuit circumvents the noise problem through the use of a technique that samples the unknown frequency at the rate of the reference signal and then averages the measured waveform with a low-pass filter.

If the input frequency f_{in} is equal to the reference f_{ref}, a nonzero average results at the output. However, if $f_{in} \neq f_{ref}$, the average of the samples is zero. In addition, the circuit is immune to noise and works well between 100 hertz and 100 kilohertz.

Comparator U_2 (a) determines the sampling frequency that is derived from reference input signal V_{ref}.

Resistor R_2 determines the duration of the sample pulse. The output of U_2 turns switch Q_1 on and off at the rate f_{ref}. The input signal, which is compared with the reference signal, is amplified by U_1 whose gain is set by R_1. Capacitor C_1 blocks any dc component of V_{in}. The cutoff frequency of the low-pass filter is determined by R_3 and C_3 and is given by the equation $f_c = 1/2\pi R_3 C_3$.

The output of the filter (b) keeps comparator U_3 in the high state as long as $|f_{in} - f_{ref}| < f_c$. The output of U_3 turns low otherwise. The response time of the circuit is determined by time constant $R_3 C_3$. To satisfy the response time and the frequency accuracy, the designer must appropriately select values for R_3 and C_3.

The harmonics of f_{ref} will also result in a nonzero average and therefore must be attenuated by adding a low-pass filter with a cutoff frequency less than $2f_{ref}$ at the input. Also, the phase delay between $V_{in}(t)$ and $V_{ref}(t)$ must not equal 90° because it will result in a zero average even when $f_{in} = f_{ref}$. Adding a phase delay to either signal will eliminate this problem. The circuit assumes that the phase difference between V_{in} and V_{ref} is less than ±90°. If no such certainty is guaranteed, a window comparator should replace U_3. □

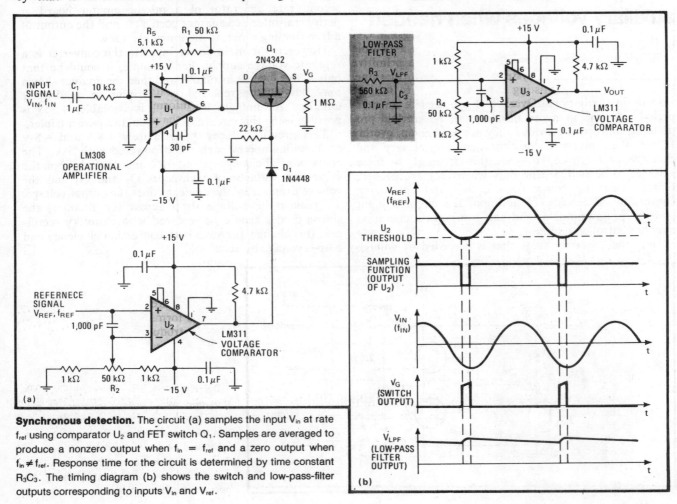

Synchronous detection. The circuit (a) samples the input V_{in} at rate f_{ref} using comparator U_2 and FET switch Q_1. Samples are averaged to produce a nonzero output when $f_{in} = f_{ref}$ and a zero output when $f_{in} \neq f_{ref}$. Response time for the circuit is determined by time constant $R_3 C_3$. The timing diagram (b) shows the switch and low-pass-filter outputs corresponding to inputs V_{in} and V_{ref}.

Recovering the clock pulse from NRZ-inverted data

by Doug Manchester
Halcyon, San Jose, Calif.

Although most data networks use nonreturn-to-zero–inverted encoding for the incoming data stream, few interface devices can recover a data-rate clock pulse from an NRZI source. However, this NRZI encoding and decoding circuit is capable of recovering not only that kind of clock pulse but also a data-rate clock pulse for synchronous data from an asynchronous modem.

An exclusive-NOR gate and a D-type flip-flop help turn serial binary data into NRZI data. The encoder truth table (Fig. 1a) shows that D_t is the binary data that is encoded at time t, Q_t is the state of the encoder output at time t, and Q_{t+1} is the state of the encoder output at the next bit time.

The NRZI data can be decoded by the circuit in Fig. 1b. This circuit performs the inverse of the encoding function and extracts the relevant information from the received encoded data. The clock frequency is synchronized with the clock pulse used for encoding the data.

The clock-pulse recovery circuit (c) uses a 4-bit counter u_1 to generate the bit-rate clock from the received data and the circuit clock that is 16 times clock$_1$. The counter is reset on every edge transition of data. The received data is sampled in the bit center for maximum distortion tolerance. Distortion as high as 2% per bit for 25 bits is tolerated without resynchronization. The master reset (MR) does not occur on a rising clock-pulse edge (d), for if it rose just prior to that rising edge, clock$_1$ would occur $1/16$ of a bit before the bit center. □

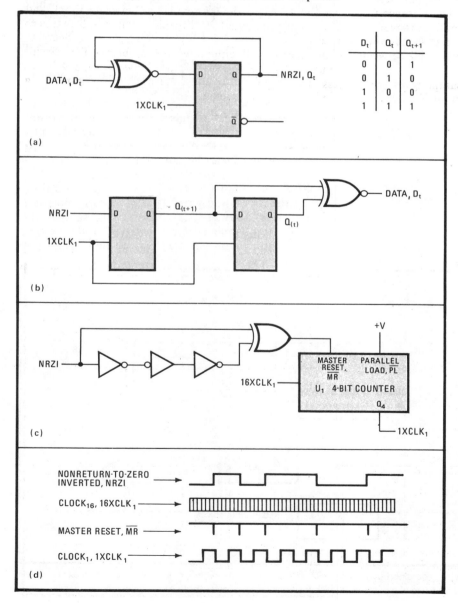

D_t	Q_t	Q_{t+1}
0	0	1
0	1	0
1	0	0
1	1	1

Recovery. Using the logic in (a), the binary data is encoded into NRZI data. This NRZI data can be decoded by performing the inverse of encoding function (b). The clock is recovered from the received data by the 4-bit counter U_1 that is clocked at 16 times the fundamental clock$_1$ (c). A typical timing diagram is depicted in (d).

Pulse-width discriminator eliminates unwanted pulses

by George Raffoul
Lockheed Engineering & Management Services Co., Houston, Texas

In many digital communications systems, nonreturn-to-zero data is converted into the biphase type before transmission because the receiver can then recover clock information embedded within the data through phase-locked-loop techniques. Unfortunately, the biphase data is noisy since the NRZ data is rarely (if ever) in phase with the transmitter clock (Fig. 1a). These unwanted chirps may be silenced by including a pulse-width discriminator in the receiver block (Fig. 1b).

The circuit (Fig. 2a) eliminates the undesired pulses by slightly delaying the biphase pulse. The 0-to-1 transition of the noisy data triggers one-shot U_{2-a}, which produces pulses at its Q and $\bar{Q}$ outputs, respectively. To compensate for U_{2-a}'s turn-on delay, the positive pulse is switched through exclusive-OR gates U_{3-a} and U_{3-b} and delayed by about 150 nanoseconds.

If the 0-to-1 transition in the input signal represents the leading edge of a pulse that is longer than U_{2-a}'s pulse width—400 ns for the components shown—the AND gate U_{4-b}'s output is a 150-ns pulse. However, if this 0-to-1 transition in the input represents the leading edge of a pulse that is shorter than U_{2-a}'s pulse width, U_{4-b} produces no output. Thus the output of U_{4-b} sets latch U_5 whenever a pulse of desired width is detected.

Similarly, one-shot U_{2-b} is triggered by a 1-to-0 transition of the input, and gates U_{3-c} and U_{3-d} compensate for the turn-on delay of U_{2-b}. AND gate U_{4-c} samples the inverse of the input signal for a duration of 400 ns, and U_{4-d} produces a narrow pulse if the input signal is greater

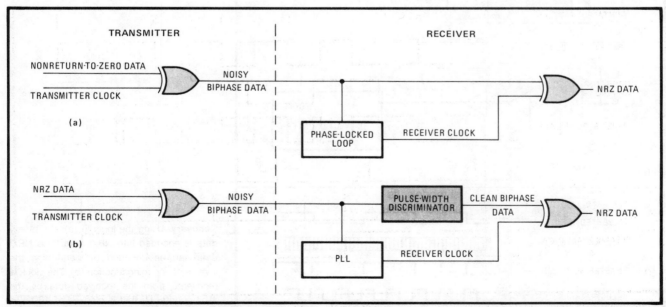

1. Biphase data. At the transmitter, biphase data is obtained by passing NRZ data and the transmitter clock signal through an exclusive-OR gate (a). This data is noisy and therefore requires the use of a pulse-width discriminator in the receiver (b) to eliminate unwanted pulses.

than $\overline{Q}$ output of U_{2-b}.

The narrow pulse output of U_{4-d} resets RS latch U_5. The timing diagram (Fig. 2b) shows narrow pulses at the outputs of U_{4-b} and U_{4-d} along with a clean biphase waveform at the Q output of U_5. The figure shows that the data is now free of undesired pulses a, b, c, d, and e, but delayed by an amount equal to the one-shot's pulse width. This width is adjusted by proper selection of the one-shot's RC time constant. □

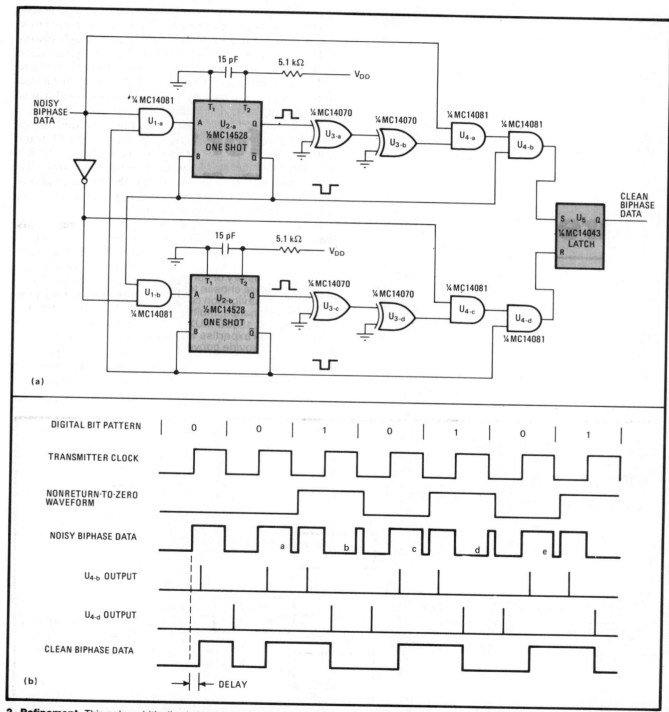

2. Refinement. This pulse-width discriminator circuit uses two one-shots, an RS latch, and a few exclusive-OR and AND gates to eliminate undesired pulses from biphase data (a). The timing diagram (b) shows that the unwanted pulses a, b, c, d, and e are the result of a delay between NRZ data and the transmitter clock signal. The clean output data is delayed.